MW01518663

When God Calls

A Biography of Bishop Arthur M. Brazier

When God Calls

A Biography
of
Bishop Arthur M. Brazier

Dr. Sammie M. Dortch

William B. Eerdmans Publishing Company

Grand Rapids, Michigan
Cambridge, England

Copyright © 1996

William B. Eerdmans Publishing Company
255 Jefferson Ave. SE Grand Rapids, MI 49503 /
P.O. Box 163 Cambridge CB3 9PU U.K.

All rights reserved
Printed in the United States of America

Library of Congress Cataloging-in-Publication Data

To the people of the Apostolic Church of God who,
when I was in doubt, reminded me that the writing
of this book was indeed a task that I had been
called to undertake and to complete.

Table of Contents

Acknowledgments

No written work is exclusively the creation of the writer. It usually results from much study and personal reflection and sometimes from hours of informal dialogue with many people. Such dialogue provides threads of thought that must later be woven together into the tapestry of the whole piece. For the bits and pieces of this book I owe special thanks to the many "saints" (a name affectionately used by the members of the Apostolic Church of God when they refer to each other) whose names I do not know. They repeatedly greeted me, a stranger in their midst, with "Praise the Lord!" and often fell into step with me as we walked the long corridor that connects the Kenwood sanctuary (old church) to the Dorchester sanctuary (new church). Their actions spoke more loudly than their words that the Apostolic Church of God is a "big church with a little church inside."

The influence of the following persons during the gestation and subsequent birthing process of this book deserves particular acknowledgment. Alfonzo Thurman, professor of leadership and educational-policy studies and dean of education, Northern Illinois University, encouraged me to write the book when it was just a thought. He also read and made copious written comments during the book's various stages of development. David Daniels, assistant professor of church history, McCormick Theological Seminary, raised questions early on that forced me to rethink the direction of the book. Kenneth Smith, president of Chicago Theological Seminary, read the manuscript and reinforced the idea that Bishop Arthur Monroe Brazier indeed had traveled a path that was worth sharing with others who might be struggling with their own call. Dorothy Reed, a dedicated friend who, fortunately for me, is also knowledgeable about Scripture, was never too busy to find an undergirding scriptural reference for an idea. Jean Brannon, another friend, gave much needed editorial direction as I labored over the revisions requested by the editor and publisher. Gerald Knuckolls, a deacon in the Apostolic Church of God, patiently answered many of my naive questions about the Pentecostal worship experience. Assistant pastor Elder Larry Martin, who often "walks" with Bishop Brazier and mirrors the humility of his mentor, was never too busy to assist during the data-gathering process. Finally, two women at the Apostolic Church of God — Doris Williams, receptionist, and Julia Clark, Bishop Brazier's secretary — provided me with what a stranger needs when entering into an unknown experience — warmth and a sense of place, in this case, a place among the people of God.

There are three other persons to whom I feel indebted: the publisher, William Eerdmans, Jr., who was able to see the potential of a book in spite of the roughness of the first manuscript version; the editor, Jeanne Ambrose, whose frankness ultimately led to my writing a much improved book; and the project developer, Sandra DeGroot, whose soothing reassurance during the last stages of the revisions kept me believing that "this too would pass."

Even with all this support, any mistakes that remain are mine.

Preface

The reasons we start on a particular path can sometimes change during the course of the journey. This is exactly what happened in my interaction with Bishop Arthur Monroe Brazier. My conversations with Bishop Brazier took on a dimension that I never anticipated when I interviewed him for a research project I was conducting. At the end of the project, I had a nagging feeling there was still some "unfinished business" between us. This new work with Bishop Brazier has brought about a sense of completion.

Bishop Brazier was one of several men I interviewed during a study of African American men and their feelings of alienation from American society. The underlying question was whether men who occupy a place in society that is viewed as "successful" have a different sense of alienation than men who live on the fringes of society do. The men viewed as living on the fringes saw themselves as having survived a journey into the bowels of the earth because they felt a kinship with what they called "the Holy Spirit." They described it as "that which was not me, that which was a higher power." However, they indicated that in spite of this entity that kept them alive, there was something painfully missing in their lives — "spiritually present" fathers. This absence was at the center of their feelings of alienation and aloneness in society. The successful men, on the other hand, described an inner journey into the caverns of their own beings, where they discovered something which could keep their spirits alive and give them what theologian Paul Tillich called "the courage to be."

After I had written the side of the story that spoke about the alienation and pain that grow out of loneliness and isolation and about the rage resulting from lack of spiritually present father figures, it seemed at some barely conscious level that the project was incomplete without the inclusion of more than a cursory description of a man who had had a spiritually present father and who himself represented such a model for his children, not to mention the children of thousands of others and people in general who sought mentoring or pastoring from him. Even though I did not know it at the time, it was this vague sense of incompleteness that was central to bringing me back to Bishop Arthur Brazier, a man who had internalized the Holy Spirit and had moved beyond survival into a rich life of sharing, caring, and loving.

Suffice it to say, in Bishop Brazier I have neither sought nor found a perfect man. Instead I found one who, in answering the call of God, grew to understand many of its expectations, a man who, though recognizing that he is set apart, also realizes that he is still required to be authentically humble in the presence of the persons to whom Jesus devoted his work, the "disinherited." In essence, in Bishop Arthur Monroe Brazier I found a man who struggles daily to understand the Christian life and to live what he believes.

Introduction

One Path: Past, Present, and Future ... life,
indeed all experience, is heavy with
meaning, with particular significance.
 — *Howard Thurman*

Bishop Arthur Brazier's life journey demonstrates that we
can transcend the barriers and limitations externally
imposed upon us by the circumstances in which we are
born. His journey suggests that those who overcome
adverse circumstances often ultimately enjoy enriched
personal lives and, in the long run, make a significant
impact upon the lives of people who have been relegated
to living on the margins of the society — the disinherited.

Bishop Brazier has lived through the indignities and
horrors of racial segregation without losing his spirit or
giving up the message that was given to him for God's
people. He has not survived because he has cloistered
himself within the hallowed walls of the cathedral,
dedicating himself to theological ponderings, or because
he has limited his role to serving only the people who
worship in the massive congregation he serves. His
ministry is intricately interwoven with the threads of a
social-justice philosophy. Bishop Brazier's particular
ministry is broader than caring only for the souls of
people. His voice, for example, can be heard, along with
other voices, giving leadership to the idea that the urban

community that works is one that attracts economically, culturally, and socially diverse people because it provides housing at various economic levels — low-cost to moderately expensive.

What is most important about Bishop Brazier is that the piece of black church history that Bishop Brazier has influenced and created will be available to others long after he ceases to bring the message he has been given. The message given to this man should be remembered, because he, like others — Martin Luther King Jr., Vernon Johns, Howard Thurman, Adam Clayton Powell — was called to challenge believers to change the quality of their lives. These leaders were not just ministers called to preach the gospel. They were called into the fullness of what it means to "do" theology, to preach, to teach, to live the Word in spiritual and social-justice contexts. They were also men who were spiritually present to those whom they served.

The wisdom Bishop Brazier gained by reflecting upon his knowledge and experience is the heart of what is captured on the pages that follow. This book is not intended to provide a formula for those who are seeking a greater understanding of how a person moves from hearing to heeding the call. Instead, it is a sharing of some of the philosophical, theological, and political strategies that may be helpful to anyone who is willing to take the risks necessary to lead God's people. Such a person, like Bishop Brazier, must give up the unexamined preaching of the gospel, the willingness to do almost anything in order to remain popular with the "worldy contemporary churches," and any refusal to see why mainline churches are losing members to the historically fundamentalist churches.

It is important to note that Bishop Brazier is considered "progressive" by some of his detractors. This criticism seems to be related to his affiliation with the Pentecostal Assemblies of the World (P.A.W.) and his veering from some traditional Pentecostal doctrines. He makes a clear distinction between "traditional" (how we have historically acted) and "scriptural" interpretations (how it is written that we are to act). In spite of many spirited discussions, Bishop Brazier has chosen to remain with the P.A.W. "We are in agreement on so many other issues," he says. "There has been no effort on the part [of the leadership] of the P.A.W. to coerce me into silence or to change my point of view. I am free to speak what is laid on my heart by the Word." This book portrays the undeniably significant contributions of an African American man. Even more significantly, it intends to honor the Holy Spirit as the source of that man's life and work. While the focus of the book is on a specific man at a specific time, the message is universally appropriate for all times.

Bishop Brazier has the distinction of being like the mythical Roman god Janus, looing in two directions at the same time, backward to the time in which he was born and forward toward the time known as tomorrow. Like many others who share this distinction, he moves with agility between the time zones. Yet he recognizes that he should not go faster or farther than the people whom he serves can comprehend.

When asked to reflect upon moving forward and making changes, he simply says, "I have a sense of the congregation; there are times when I must patiently wait before I move." He sees his response as being anchored in a belief that the power of the Holy Spirit allows him simultaneously to see the vision and to know when the people are ready to hear the message.

How can one function as a integrated person when he is constantly torn between the present and the future, between yesterday, today, and tomorrow? The answer for Bishop Brazier lies in the fact that what he lives and what he teaches are firmly grounded in Scripture — which does not change over time. The visionary in Bishop Brazier frequently "sees" the possibilities of what can be, but the grounded one who shares the same inner space knows that the ancient wisdom requires him to "wait upon word from the Lord" before acting upon that which his intellect foresees as the creative answer to a problem facing the people.

Bishop Brazier advocates a holistic approach to the people he serves, ministering to them in word and deed. As he responds to the call of God, he struggles to live according to the Word, not in order to be saved but because he is saved. As he puts it, "It is impossible for [one] who has tasted the Holy Spirit to be unsaved or lost .... We are looking forward to the glorious appearing of our savior Jesus Christ .... We should be careful about the life we live as Christians not in order to be save — we already are — but because we are saved."

Like theologian Karl Barth, Bishop Brazier views the goal of theological work as service to God and man, and, like Barth, he believes that nothing can be accomplished in the realm of the religious, moral, intellectual, or spiritual without the will of God. Even when theologians are good and faithful, Barth and Brazier would both say, they are still human; therefore, they must depend upon God's grace to live.

Finally, like Barth, Bishop Brazier is of the opinion that because humans are sinful by nature, no one is in a position to consider him- or herself "famous" or a "theological genius," no matter how phenomenal the growth in his or her congregation is. The theologian instead is admonished to listen humbly to the voices of the church fathers and of contemporary theologians, demonstrating an "openness to the world."

The humility of Bishop Brazier is most obvious when he is in the presence of those who attempt to elevate "the called one" or in the presence of those who choose to accept such elevation as appropriate recognition of their religious life. He displays great discomfort when he is set apart from others because of the size of the congregation he pastors or the profundity of his sermons. He quickly reminds the speaker that "I, like others, am not free from sin or error, but it is by the grace of God that I am able to do what I do. The Scripture leaves no room for doubt in this matter: 'For by grace are ye saved through faith; and that not of yourselves: it is the gift of God.' I look in wonderment at what the Holy Spirit has directed me to do in his name!"

Bishop Brazier clearly sees the importance of not being oblivious to the world. However, for him, the sense of "openness to the world" does not give a person license to do whatever he or she pleases. He says, "Let me make it perfectly clear: the life of a born-again believer changes. His or her desire is to obey God …. Therefore, the person strives to do so, but we all fall short."

The content of this book is a result of hearing Bishop Brazier's journey partly in his own words and partly in the words of those around him. Literature of various kinds is also interspersed where relevant. The scriptural references are taken from the *New Scofield Reference Bible,* 1967, Authorized King James Version.

The Man

Before the Call

According as he hath chosen us in him before
the foundation of the world, that we should be
holy and without blame before him, in love.
— *Ephesians 1:4*

From all outward appearances, Arthur Monroe Brazier
entered the world with few visible signs foretelling the
service he would render unto humankind in answering the
call of the Holy Spirit. Nothing in his family background
prepared him for the leadership position he holds as
pastor of the twelve-thousand-member congregation of
the Apostolic Church of God in Chicago. Nor did his early
experiences indicate he would be prepared to serve as the
bishop of a district while participating as a leader in social-
justice movements — housing, community organizing,
and school desegregation — in Chicago. The significance
of the stages of his journey comes to light only as the layers
of his life are peeled back. Upon close examination, we
shall see that the road he took indeed had markers, signs
of things to come. One such marker stands out in Bishop
Brazier's memory. While crossing a bustling south-side
Chicago intersection as a young boy, he was struck by a
two-ton truck but escaped completely unscathed. Perhaps
this event was an indication that God was protecting and
preparing Arthur Brazier for his important future mission.
   Many years later, when he was aware of the path he was

to travel, Bishop Brazier refused to veer from that path even when faced with a death threat. In the 1960s, as a Pentecostal pastor he initially tried to toe the line and not deviate from the traditional teachings of his denomination. However, "when I witnessed African American children being denied access to the American dream [quality education and housing], I could no longer remain silent," he says, and he became involved in the civil-rights movement, an act which was initially frowned upon by his denomination. However, he felt compelled from within not only to speak out but also to engage in actions that would correct the situation.

As a result, his life was threatened. He was working with two Chicago youth gangs, the Blackstone Rangers and the East Side Disciples, when he learned of the death threat. "There was a time during the period when I was working with the gangs that was harried," he recalls. "The head of gang intelligence received information that the gangs had put a contract out on my life. But it did not deter us from continuing to carry out our work. I had a series of confrontations with various gang leaders, but we never budged from our position that the Woodlawn Organization (TWO) was going to control the finances and the grant [awarded by the Office of Economic Opportunity]. Contrary to public opinion, I never had any trouble out of Jeff Fort, [a gang leader] who had become a rather infamous character during that period. I met with him on a number of occasions; never was threatened by him." In this, as in other situations, Bishop Brazier demonstrates how his personal charisma often soothes the disquieted spirit in others.

People flock to the Apostolic Church of God to see for themselves what their friends, family, students, and coworkers have described. One theologian, puzzled, asked, "What does he do? Why do people go there? There are so many of them." Even after one of his seminarians invited

4

him to visit, he had difficulty believing what he saw with his own eyes, particularly the number of "educated" people waving their arms and rising to their feet when they felt the Spirit move in and around them. Learned university professors and type-A businessmen and businesswomen from more sedate denominations like the United Church of Christ, the Disciples of Christ, the Roman Catholic Church, and the Progressive Church are among those who seem to relish the rather demonstrative Apostolic experience.

It is intriguing to know that some of those who come are looking for vicarious ways of sharing in whatever it is that the people at Apostolic profess to receive from the man they fondly call Bishop. Some pastors say they would like to meet with Bishop Brazier, but they hesitate to ask because "there are so many demands on his time." In part, their hesitancy is the fear of seeming foolish or naive or of being told no in the event that he would not recognize them in the procession of faces he must see in a day. Yet the graciousness and humility of his seemingly untiring spirit greets them at the door when they do have the courage to let him know they are among the many.

Although Bishop Brazier's congregation has twelve thousand members, he is available to anyone who requests a telephone or in-person visit. He personally schedules his appointments, returns telephone calls, and greets worshipers after each of the services. Bishop Brazier sees nothing complex in what is drawing the diverse congregation to the church. He says that "Pentecostalism is not just for the 'disinherited.' We are preaching a message that middle-class people also long to hear — that we are saved by grace and grace alone. When one accepts this tenet, he or she can begin to live a new life, a life under grace. There is an incomparable joy in this experience."

2

The Early Years

When I was a child, I spoke as a child, I
understood as a child, I thought as a child ....
— *1 Corinthians 13:11*

Arthur Monroe Brazier was born in the Hyde Park
community of Chicago — an academic and cultural center
that flourished because of the presence and influence of
the prestigious University of Chicago. "I was born," he says,
"on July 22, 1921, in a third-floor apartment at 5210 South
Lake Park Avenue. I was born in those days in which very
few African Americans were admitted to hospitals due to
the racial climate. There were only two hospitals black
people could go to in Chicago — Provident and Cook
County. Consequently, most of us were born at home."

The community was lush with tree-lined streets and
large comfortable homes. Though African Americans were
no strangers to the community, their numbers were made
up mostly of domestics and hotel employees.

Arthur was born to parents who would not be
considered young. His mother, Geneva Brazier, was born
in 1885 and was 36 when he was born. His father, Robert
Brazier, was born in 1873 and was 48 when Arthur, his
youngest child, arrived. Between them, his parents had five
children. His mother brought two children to the union —
Lonnie, who was nine years older than Arthur, and Minnie.
Carrie and Jessie were his father's children. These siblings,

7

who were twelve to fifteen years older than Arthur, were born in Birmingham, Alabama, from where the Braziers migrated to Chicago.

"They [his mother and father] met in Alabama in a little town called Montevallo about twenty miles outside of Birmingham. It is my recollection," says the Bishop, "that my father was trapped in a mining disaster. He vowed that if he got out of the mine, he would never go back again. The other miners returned. My mother couldn't understand why my father didn't go back to the mine. Instead, he came to Chicago. That was in 1917. He later sent for my mother and three of the older children: Minnie, Lonnie, and Carrie. I was born in 1921."

The social climate of the Chicago into which young Brazier was born was one where racial tensions had escalated because African Americans had gradually moved past the invisible boundaries that for a long time had separated the black community from the white community. African American families were moving into homes that had been previously occupied by white families. White Hyde Parkers experienced this as an invasion and worked diligently to drive the black families out of the community.

Young Arthur seems to have been insulated from the feelings and the retaliations that erupted around the struggle for housing. His parents did not discuss racism in their home. Nonetheless, he was not immune to the historical reality and the suffering of others.

"There was no talk of racial conflict in my home," he says. "In fact, my parents never expressed any bitterness or animosity toward white people at all. Consequently, I was not raised to harbor bitterness. My first real taste of racial prejudice or discrimination came during my Army career."

As with most of the significant events in his life, Bishop Brazier's own words depict the Chicago scene: "Although we lived in a segregated system in Chicago, I never came into conflict with a lot of white animosity. The vestiges of open segregation were not clearly seen in the sense that you had to ride in the back of the bus. There were no separate drinking fountains; you were treated with courtesy in department stores downtown; you did not have to go in side doors or back doors to go to the movies, or sit in the balcony. These obvious blatant signs of discrimination were not there."

Young Brazier's beginning, like that of many blacks, was meager. He describes his home as "a calm household with very little arguing. My father instilled a certain amount of fear in me when I heard his voice raised." He sees his father as a great man — "kindness was at [his] core. He raised his voice maybe two times each year. My mother was the disciplinarian, and my father spoiled me. He was a family man who brought his money home and gave it to my mother."

Bishop Brazier says he "felt torn between" his mother's and his father's ways. His mother was assertive; she made decisions and got things done.

"She did everything she could to help people. As poor as we were, she would buy other families shoes so that their little children could go to Sunday school. My mother worked as a domestic, and often the families for whom she worked gave their old clothes to her. She picked them up in the car and brought them home. Then she sorted them, and certain kinds of things we would get, and certain kinds of things she would save for some family in the church that needed clothing. Even though we wanted them, she would say, 'No, you can't have this. This is going to Sister Jones or the family of Brother Williams.' She reached out to people, and I think that's where I got that particular thrust."

Bishop Brazier credits his mother with being responsible for his religious development and his father with emphasizing fair treatment. He feels that he has struck a balance between the best both parents had to offer.

Geneva Brazier dedicated her life to service. She established her own "alms" program in her home, through which she gathered clothing and distributed it to poor people. Her primary job at the time was "taking in white people's washing or going into their homes to wash," Bishop Brazier says.

Geneva Brazier was saved in 1920. "She was saved the year before I was born," Bishop Brazier says. "To give you some idea about her, she tried to conform to the religion [Pentecostalism] and not be openly rebellious while at the same time realizing that some of the worshipers were really sort of on the fringes. For example, they taught against Christmas trees. It had something to do with the pagan practice of cutting down trees in the forest and fashioning idols out of them. We never had a Christmas tree in our house." As the Bishop tells the story, it is clear that this was not a disturbing experience for him.

"I never knew why and never asked why, but we had a long couch, and on Christmas Eve that couch would be covered with white linen, and all the gifts would be placed on that couch or on the floor around it. The couch would be sprinkled with icicles and everything else that went on a Christmas tree, except lights; so the couch became our Christmas tree. There were a lot of children in the house, and on Christmas morning we headed for the couch. I never understood this [the prohibition against Christmas trees] until I was an adult and in the church, where I heard these people preaching against trees. Growing up, no one said anything about trees. As far as I was concerned, this was normal." (Bishop Brazier got his first Christmas tree in 1951, several years after he was married and with his wife, Esther Isabel, and children had moved into their first apartment. Neither he nor his wife was bound by the tradition that teaches against Christmas trees.)

Eventually, Geneva Brazier became the pastor of Universal Church of Christ in Chicago — by default. At the time, Arthur was 14. The congregation was a "house church" at 4107 South Michigan. When the pastor got into a doctrinal dispute with the congregation, the people rejected him and asked Geneva Brazier to take over the church.

Bishop Brazier recalls his mother's feelings about the way some people regarded the church: "My mother felt hurt because some insensitive people referred to the church as a 'garbage can' because of her more liberal practice of not turning people away from church because of some human weaknesses they may have had, such as wearing earrings or smoking cigarettes. The church had no artificial walls; anybody would attend. She had strong convictions and tried her very best to help people who had what Pentecostals referred to as 'weaknesses' and 'carnality' in those days."

Bishop Brazier's father, Robert Brazier, was a maintenance man at the Hyde Park Laundry Company in Chicago from 1921 until 1940. He worked eight to ten hours a day and was earning twenty-eight dollars a week when he retired.

Bishop Brazier remembers his father as "a very laid-back person. He was not a man who expressed a great deal of emotion. The greatest emotion I ever saw my father display was when I told him I had been drafted into the Army. He cried when I left. The next great emotional display occurred when I came home from the Army. That was December 28, 1945."

Robert Brazier was saved after an incident in which his young son saw him falter. The Bishop remembers, "It was his birthday, May 30, 1928 — Memorial Day. It sticks in my mind so vividly because I saw him drinking. I was in another room, he was back in the kitchen, and I looked back there and saw him with a bottle turned up to his mouth. You know, in 1928 it was bathtub gin; it was bootleg whiskey because Prohibition was in effect.

"My dad took me to Jackson Park. Evidently it had been raining because when my father fell, he fell in a puddle of water alongside the street. Through my tears I tried to pull him up, but I couldn't. These men stopped and picked him up and put us both in a car and took us home. I can remember him looking up at me in such a way that I haven't forgotten that look …. I never saw my father drunk ever again. It was at that time that he started going to church. The pastor was a man by the name of Alexander R. Schooler."

It is clear that his father was not the only one influenced by this event. Arthur M. Brazier was 6 at the time, yet sixty-seven years later he still remembers the name of the pastor of the church his father joined.

"My father and I were very, very close," he says. "To see my dad walk outside in the summertime just to get fresh air was a surprise. I would run to catch up and walk with him. He would take me to the zoo or to buy my mother a present. For example, in those days on Mother's Day you had to buy your mother a flower — white if her mother was dead and red if she was alive."

During Arthur Brazier's youth there was no real separation between blacks because of their social or economic status; therefore, he remembers being exposed to the full range of black life. "In my early life the city of Chicago was covered by restrictive covenants, which meant that there were whole neighborhoods in which black people could not rent, could not buy," he says. "Black people were therefore consigned to specific geographic areas no matter what their station in life, principally what we call the west side and the south side. However, as more black people moved into Chicago, the black community merely expanded. For the most part, there was an intermingling of income groups so that a family or three, four, or five families who were on relief, which is called welfare today, in a particular block could be living nextdoor to a school teacher or across the street from a social worker or down the block from a person who was working in the stockyard. You did not have the enclaves of poverty like those created by government housing projects, where anywhere between 80 and 90 percent of the people living in a housing project might be on welfare. That was unheard of in my youth."

He remembers these early years as an exciting time in which his family provided a wonderful atmosphere. Several generations shared the same household. "We lived in a ten- or eleven-room house. My mother and father, my sister and her husband and their three children, my aunt and her two children, a cousin, another couple whose names I have forgotten, and I shared the house. The eleven rooms were filled to capacity at all times. I can never remember coming into that house and finding it totally and completely empty."

In spite of the number of people sharing the home, the family still experienced financial struggles. Bishop Brazier recalls that "everybody worked. There was no one living at home who wasn't working. They paid a little rent for their rooms to my mother. That's how my parents paid the rent for the house. They did not own it."

These struggles may almost have been welcomed. Bishop Brazier remembers being quite pleased at 16 to be rescued from attending Sunday school and church by his getting a job as a milkman's helper. "While I was raised in the Apostolic faith, it had no real meaning to me. There was nothing in it that had any appeal to me as a teenager. It was always 'don't.' There were so many things that you could not do. As innocent as shooting marbles was, young people could not even do that."

These early restrictive experiences, coupled with his mother's somewhat liberal spirit and his own questing spirit, may have been formative influences on his "progressive" version of Pentecostalism. Within him there was often a curiosity that pushed him to search for answers that went beyond that which could be readily seen or explained. There was also an independence that led him early on to develop a strong work ethic.

"When I reached an age where I could get a job on a milk wagon — it was during the Depression — I did," he says. "This meant that I had money in my pocket and did not have to ask my father for money. He always tried to see to it that I had some kind of money even during the midst of the Depression, when men really had nothing. My father left me fifteen cents under the scarf on the dresser every day. Once in a while I would ask for an extra dime, which would allow me to go to a restaurant before I went to a movie. I could get a bowl of rice and beans and a cup of coffee for a dime at Foote's at 35th and State Street. It was next door to the State Theater.

"Money was important in our lives. There were times when we had trouble keeping the lights on. The light bill was very low, but sometimes there was no money to pay it. So my mother would say, 'Don't let the light man in,' or 'Don't let the gas man in.' During that period you had to get inside the house to cut this stuff off.

"I remember that there were times when my father had to borrow money from the place where he was employed — borrowing money was, I assume, what we today call getting an advance on your salary — in order to buy coal.

"My mother worked, taking in laundry. I remember her saying she was very thankful to the Lord because, no matter how hard things were, we never had to go on relief. That was a source of pride to her."

Bishop Brazier believes that in a way his parents' allowing him to miss Sunday school may have been related to his working and beginning to contribute to the household.

Young Brazier also left Wendell Phillips High School at this time in spite of his parents' pleas for him to remain in school and to graduate. (He had graduated from Douglas, a predominantly black elementary school.) Due to segregation, all the working black men he saw were "running on the road" (working for railroads in the capacity of Pullman-car porters or dining-room waiters) or sweeping up hair from barbershop floors.

At that time he did not see much of a future, even with an education. "I regretted that decision. I had to work hard to educate myself for years after that," he says.

There have been times when Bishop Brazier considered sharing his early experiences with young people, particularly as his experiences relate to developing a work ethic regardless of one's educational level. However, he was occasionally admonished to remember that this bittersweet memory could be misleading to late twentieth-century youth. Bishop Brazier recalls a discussion he had in the 1970s with Barbara Sizemore, who was then the director of the Woodlawn Experimental School District. Her primary focus was on upgrading education. "Barbara's concern was that if I told them that I did not finish high school, it might be a reason to cause some of them to decide that high school was not necessary, and that would certainly misrepresent my thinking on the matter," he says.

"With formal education, I think I could have done more. However, I know that I am where I am because of the Lord. Sometimes I am astounded at where the Lord has brought me, a high-school dropout."

He shares a story that illustrates his life-long pursuit of learning." Attorney Allison Davis and I went to London on a work-study project for the Ford Foundation in 1973. We were looking at how Londoners provided housing for the poor. We hopped over to Paris. I was really mesmerized by the language. I could not speak a word of it. I said to myself, when I get back home, I think I'm going to learn this language. I was there three days, and when I came back to Chicago, I enrolled in Berlitz Language Center and learned to speak French. My wife couldn't understand this. She wanted to know if I planned to move to France. I got into the language because I wanted to learn it. I felt that it was a cultural thing. It helped me to begin to understand another country, its culture, its kings, the revolution — all of this while learning a new language. It gave me a sense of accomplishment."

During the summers of 1933 and 1934, when young Brazier was 12 and 13, he parked cars for ten cents per car at the Chicago World's Fair. Remnants of the early value he put on a good work ethic can be seen throughout his life. The only job he recalls being fired from was that of dishwasher — "I was too slow."

When Arthur was 17, he worked as a delivery boy for Coles Drug Store on 47th and Lake Park. "It was at this point that my concept of my snug world changed, and I found myself thrust into the social and political realities of the broader society. My response was one of fear for the fate of black men because they were being executed by white men. It was my knowledge of a 1919 race riot that kindled the fear."

On July 27, 1919, the struggle over the inadequate housing situation in Chicago culminated in one of the worst race riots in American history. Eugene Williams drowned at 29th Street on the Southside Beach after reportedly being stoned by whites. The ignoring of the charges by the police ignited the long-simmering racial tension. Twenty people were killed, and hundreds were injured.

"The fear of the eruption, at any time, of racial tension was further heightened by the news of the lynching of black men in the South," Bishop Brazier says. "Lynchings were commonplace during the thirties. These fears were exacerbated when my job [at the time] required me to ride my bike through white neighborhoods in Hyde Park. After four months of travel through hostile territory, working a four-to-midnight shift, I quit the job.

"I think that the fear stood out in my mind because of what I read in the newspapers about the animosity of whites against blacks in the South and because we lived in such a segregated system in Chicago. Although I never came into conflict with a lot of white animosity, I had a serious fear about being attacked in white neighborhoods at night. Almost all apartment buildings required that deliveries be made at the rear, and the thought of a young black meandering around in a white neighborhood in dark alleys was a little more than I could take; not that anyone ever attacked me, but the thought of it and the fear of what could happen and how I could be mistaken for a robber or murderer or someone who would be prowling around to attack white women was more than I could stand. Therefore, I didn't think the job was worth that kind of aggravation!"

After that, he worked sporadically for approximately two years as a delivery boy. He was a helper on a Bowman Dairy Company milk truck. Black people were not regularly hired by the company. However, Bishop Brazier reports that it was not unusual for the regular milkmen to hire and to pay black helpers out of their own pockets because of the rigors of door-to-door milk deliveries.

By 1940 he was employed at the place where his father worked, the Hyde Park Laundry, where he earned fifteen dollars a week as an elevator operator. "You can imagine the joy I had in doing this relatively easy job for fifteen dollars per week. It was the first job I had that was of any consequence. I had worked earlier as a paper baler for seven dollars a month in the laundry. I would pick up wrapping paper and bale it. Then once a month I would have enough to sell to the man who came around picking up scrap paper," the Bishop remembers.

Since that time he has never been unemployed. He says, "I wanted to help out by earning my own money. I tried to get on the WPA (Works Progress Administration) and the CCC (Civilian Conservation Corps) — relief or emergency work programs initiated by President Franklin Roosevelt's New Deal to provide employment during the Depression years. Because my father had a job, I was not eligible. So I asked my father if he would sign me up for the Eighth Regiment, a black Army Reserve unit at 35th and Giles. He said no — emphatically. Because I was under age, I could not join on my own. He said, 'Son, I'm not going to sign because if a war breaks out [I guess it was 1938 or 1939], you will be the first one to go.'"

Having older parents may have been part of the impetus that spurred young Brazier into developing an early sense of maturity and responsibility and may have reinforced the idea that these qualities have their own rewards. Watching the way his parents approached work provided a measure by which he began to develop some sense of the importance of work. Young Brazier was no stranger to work. He sought work even though it was not required, because it allowed him to have a sense of autonomy even within a nurturing family structure.

It is obvious that his parents etched an indelible impression upon the very core of his young being, so much so that some sixty years after boyhood he recalls with great acuity the lessons they taught. Geneva and Robert Brazier modeled what it meant for saved people to hear the Word given to them by the God of the gospel. Young Brazier also had an opportunity to observe the ways in which his parents' spirits remained unencumbered and unbroken by the conditions of their time.

Bishop Brazier seems to have received from his parents the essence of what he needed for his foray into the world. For him, this initial preparation or incubation process in all likelihood occurred at the unconscious level. Did the Holy Spirit lay claim on him at the outset of his life, guiding him unscathed through the poverty, racism, and brokenness that can be internalized when one is relegated by society to live a marginalized existence? It seems that a combination of forces were at work: a community of caring people and the guidance of the Holy Spirit. These influences exposed young Brazier to respect, courage, and love. He chose to internalize these instead of the influences that might have made him see himself as a black man imprisoned by a world not of his making. If you add to these influences his avid pursuit of reading (he got a library card when he was 11 or 12), it is clear that his perspective was further broadened and deepened because he saw the world through words long before he was in a position to travel. His questing after knowledge made him ripe for the intellectual development that is essential to spiritual and personal growth. He well remembers watching his father read and following his example: "My dad would get off the streetcar with the daily papers in his arms. He would come home and sit in his rocking chair, and he did not leave that chair until it was time to go to bed or to the washroom or to eat dinner. When he came home in the evening, I knew exactly where my father would be. I would sit on his lap, and he would read the paper. He would read the Herald Examiner, the Chicago American, the Chicago Tribune, the Chicago Sun, the Chicago Times, and the Chicago Daily News from front to back every day.

"I would read the Saturday Evening Post, Liberty, and Life Magazine. Those were the magazines I could afford. I went to the library and got books. I read Huckberry Finn and Tarzan the Ape Man, and I devoured Sherlock Holmes. As I grew older, I began to read books like King's Row and the novels by the Bronte sisters. I mostly read novels.

"In the fifties I began to read other writers. I became interested in Dostoevski, Sartre, Camus, and a host of others. I tried to read Paradise Lost, but I could not really get with that. Since I dropped out of high school my first year, I was trying to educate myself."

Brazier's efforts to educate himself were noticed by many, including Gerald Nuckolls, a deacon in the Apostolic Church of God who has known Brazier since 1947. He recalls the time when Arthur Brazier began to deepen his involvement in the life of the church. "I remember a late

Sunday afternoon in mid-October when a tall, slender man who weighed about 147 pounds came into the church [Apostolic Church of God] and sat down front. He was very intense and quiet; he was learning."

According to Deacon Nuckolls, this penchant for learning and the indwelling of the Holy Spirit are the keys behind Bishop Brazier's remaining in touch with the needs of the people while keeping his sight on the vision that has prevented the people from perishing.

Deacon Nuckolls foresaw more than forty years ago the leadership ability of (then) Elder Brazier. He was impressed with the man's "style, ability, and foresight." Consequently, when the pastor of the Apostolic Church of God resigned in 1960, Deacon Nuckolls took a leadership role in presenting a plan to the church elders to call Elder Brazier to pastor the congregation. Elder Brazier was serving at that time as the pastor of a congregation that shared space with the church where Deacon Nuckolls was a member.

"There was no plan at the time to merge the two churches [Universal Church of Christ and the Apostolic Church of God]," according to Deacon Nuckolls. They shared worship space, but they had two of everything else. Elder Brazier accepted the challenge, and on May 29, 1960, merged the two congregations with the loss of only one member. At that point the choirs and auxiliaries were combined into one. There were approximately eighty members between the two congregations."

Among the experiences that Deacon Nuckolls feels contributed significantly to Bishop Brazier's preparation for the call were the lessons he learned from his parents. He believes that Bishop Brazier's mother "taught him [Brazier] respect, leadership, and the importance of community involvement, and his father taught courage and love."

Bishop Brazier recalls two stories that illustrate the observations of Deacon Nuckolls. "It was 1941, and I thought life was good. I had a job operating the elevator at

20

the Hyde Park Laundry, and I made contributions to the household. I wanted to buy a car in the worst way. I had saved three hundred dollars, which I counted every day. My brother Lonnie, who was 29 at the time, accompanied me to a used-car dealer to buy a car.

"The car dealer telephoned my employer to check my employment reference. My employer felt that I could not afford the car and that I did not need the car. He said that I had to buy license and insurance, too. When I insisted that I would really like to buy this car, he told me I could buy the car if I wanted to, but, 'I can tell you now, when your father comes to ask to borrow money, I will not lend it to him,' and he walked away.

"He [the employer] was a paternalistic person. My father had worked for that company for a long time, and, as I said before, especially during the winter months, we needed coal, and he would get salary advances to purchase the coal."

Bishop Brazier remembers being concerned about putting his father in the position of asking for something that would be refused. He told his father about the threat. His father reassured him that proceeding with the plan to purchase the car would have no negative ramifications.

"My father was somewhat perturbed by the incident," says Bishop Brazier, "and told me that Mr. Fisher, the laundry owner, was not the only person who had money. My father's position made it clear to me that I could go ahead and buy the car, but I did not feel reassured. I did not want him to get a no [answer] if he had to borrow money. Therefore, I refused to purchase the car because I wanted to do nothing that might even remotely cause harm to my father."

Although young Brazier felt powerless and angry, his father's well-being was more important than his own feelings. "I resented [the employer's] paternalistic attitude and lost the incentive to save and [for a time] squandered my money after that," he says.

Another experience that contributed significantly to Bishop Brazier's preparation for the call relates to his mother. "At 17, I was at the 31st Street beach roasting hot dogs and marshmallows with three friends, a male and two females, when a police officer arrived and without explanation asked my height. When I gave it, the officer took me to the 27th Street police station and arrested me, again without explanation. The police officer tried to get me to confess to hitting someone with a brick. I felt the hand of God guiding me in this situation, and, although the police implied they would let me go if I confessed, my sense was that this was not what I was to do. I remained in jail for three days, from Wednesday to Friday. I was finally allowed to take a polygraph test that revealed that I was not lying. When they took me back to jail, I discovered that the actual charge was suspicion of murder. I was released on bail.

"This was the first time that I knew beyond a doubt that my mother, the disciplinarian, loved me. It was also the first and last time I saw her throw her arms around me and cry. She was not a demonstrative person; therefore this made the event the most memorable occasion in life. There was no doubt that my mother loved me! My mother was a wonderful woman. I think about my parents a lot. I look back and feel bad about some of the things I did as a kid. I caused them to worry."

3

Transformed by Love

And now abideth faith, hope, [love], these
three; but the greatest of these is [love].
— *1 Corinthians 13:13*

Over the years Bishop Brazier discovered the meaning of the
message that was beneath the lessons taught by his parents.
He gradually heard and felt this deeper message. He
discovered that this message was laced with the meaning
and the power of the Word and, even more important, that it
revealed love as a curative ingredient needed by one who
answers the call to preach, teach, or live by the Word.

This love is not the romantic version we seek after in
contemporary society. It is not the love that is sought as a
panacea to cure the emptiness felt because of what
psychologist Rollo May calls the existence of nonspecific
anxiety. As a curative ingredient love is not a feeling;
instead its properties can be clearly seen in the actions of
the one who has discovered what appears to be the
bottomless well from which such love flows. Being a
servant of the disinherited or of anyone else in need is at
the core of this curative experience. It is not the doing for
the other but the being with the other as he or she is
shown how to do for self that provides the balm that heals
or restores the ailing spirit.

Bishop Brazier has a primary principle that enables him
to demonstrate love as a curative ingredient when serving

others: he continues to walk among the people, to be accessible to them through the large and small trials and joys in their lives. In spite of the growth of his church and the unending demands within and outside its walls, anyone who wishes to have an audience with the Bishop may do so by simply calling the church and making the request, not of a receptionist but of the Bishop himself. This human touch is seen by Bishop Brazier as acknowledging, in a way that the people will understand, that he recognizes their need to "know that their pastor is there for them when they need him and not off someplace else."

The result of this kind of love can be seen in the faces of those who have worked alongside the Bishop and have seen him preach, teach, and live out the meaning of the Word in spite of challenges. They come for more; they come to learn how to access the Holy Spirit for themselves.

Often in his sermons Bishop Brazier reminds the listener that "being saved does not mean you will no longer encounter suffering or difficulties in your life. You are not exempt from the loneliness, fear, tragedy, or loss that often results in anxiety …. However, there is no end to what you can do through Christ. There is no lack in God. Why then when trouble comes are we still afraid? Because we have not come into who we are in Christ. What do we do when we are tested? Out of lack of knowledge, we are afraid. Ordinary Christians cannot understand the test. They ask the Lord 'Why me?' questions. As long as you are saved by grace, the trials will come, but those who believe will overcome."

Bishop Brazier sees nonspecific anxiety as resulting from a spiritual vacuum that cannot be filled even by personal intimacy. He agrees with the position Paul Tillich expresses in his book The Courage to Be that a personal encounter with anxiety is inescapable, a part of existence itself. For Tillich, courage (which he defines as "the power of the mind to overcome fear") allows one to exist in spite of anxiety. For Bishop Brazier, however, this power to overcome "is anchored in and accessible through one's relationship with the Holy Spirit .... When you receive the Holy Spirit, you receive power."

Bishop Brazier echoes Tillich's ideas on the origin and impact of anxiety. Both think anxiety is related to alienation or loss of a "spiritual center." Anxiety is described by Tillich as being aroused by the loss of an answer, however symbolic and indirect, to the question of the meaning of one's existence. Bishop Brazier preaches and teaches that separation and alienation from God are "the primary reason for the continued questing and unrest of people who have acquired education and material possessions."

A key to reaching people who experience emptiness and anxiety seems to be in what the apostle Paul identifies as the gifts of the spirit. Paul writes that they must be exercised in love. In 1 Corinthians 13: 1, 2, 4, and 13, he describes the kind of love Bishop Brazier has come to see, feel, experience, and share:

> Though I speak with the tongues of men and of angels, and have not [love], I am become as sounding [brass], or a tinkling cymbal .... And though I have the gift of prophecy, and understand all mysteries, and all knowledge; and though I have all faith, so that I could remove mountains, and have not [love], I am nothing .... Love suffereth long, and is kind; [love] envieth not; [love] vaunteth not itself, is not puffed up .... And now abideth faith, hope, [love], these three; but the greatest of these is [love].†

In response to the question of how he has come to know the qualitative aspects of love referred to by the apostle

---

† Note: "Love" is substituted for "charity," which is used in the King James Version. The term "love" is used in other versions, e.g., New International Version (NIV) and Revised Standard Version (RSV). "Love" is used here because it more aptly applies to Bishop Brazier.

Paul, Bishop Brazier says, "I think of my relationship with other people in terms of my call to feel their needs. This is particularly true of people who have been, or who feel they have been, rejected by others. People talk to you, and they want to know more about Christ. Sometimes their lives do not come anywhere near the life of a Christian. Unfortunately, some Christians are so ideologically bound to their doctrine that if a person does not fit it, they reject him or her. Not being ideologically pure allows me to reach out to people who find themselves without a place to worship while they struggle to strengthen their relationship with the Lord.

"If a person professes a desire to walk with the Lord but is caught in the throes of, for example, a cigarette habit, some congregations will expel him or her from the fellowship. I reach out to people who find themselves without Christian fellowship. The truth is, fundamentalists and progressives alike are all subject to the faults and frailties that afflict humanity. These are the things that we as Christians have to fight against in our lives. It's a part of the test and temptation and what we call 'being an overcomer.' If you are not tested and tried by these human frailties, then what is there to overcome? The fact that we are saved means that we have been lifted up from our frailties to a far greater degree than others, but yet we still have to wrestle with pride, lust, passion, envy, and sometimes hatred.

"There's a sermon there!" he concludes.

4

In the World

[For] many are called, but few chosen
                                — Matthew 20:16
In times past you lived a certain way; yet
once saved you are different, even when
faced with the same old problems.
                                — Arthur M. Brazier

During the time Bishop Brazier was "in the world," he
had experiences that shaped and sharpened the
ideological perspective that he embraced after the call.
He learned to base his evaluation of an event at least
partially upon the context in which it occurred. He
consciously tried to see every experience through the
eyes of the person in that situation and to judge every
situation in the light of its particular time and place.

"My first entrance into the Army was in an all-black unit.
[He served in the 2033rd Quarter Master unit (truck) attached
to the 52nd Air Service Group]. That really did not bother me
because I had been around black people all my life. However,
the first experience of racism that leaps into my mind
occurred when I was stationed in the South [Ripley,
Tennessee] and got a pass to go to town and had to ride in
the back of the bus," he recalls. The discrimination did not
end with the bus ride. "African American soldiers were
confined to a street where black people had their lounges
and nightclubs, and you did not dare venture off that street,"

he says. "You did not feel free to go anywhere you wanted to, especially since it was evening and dark. The night hours were the only times when our passes were in effect.

"I got another taste of racism in Dyersburg, Tennessee. There were two PXs [post exchanges], which were like department stores — the white one, which was a huge area, maybe forty to fifty thousand square feet, and the black one, which was eight to twelve hundred square feet. Obviously there was a great disparity.

"I also ran into racism in the USOs [United Service Organization], especially in the South, where it was clear that colored [African Americans were called colored or Negro at that time] soldiers were not welcome in some of what were called white USOs. In fact in Charleston there was a white USO, and there was a colored USO. We went to the colored USO. The longer I stayed in the Army, the more I became aware of segregation and how we were rigidly separated in the Army.

"A dentist once called me a nigger. I felt helplessness, powerlessness, and rage in that situation. I think about it like it happened yesterday. What could I have done? I felt a deep sense of anger about the way black men were treated in the Army. This segregation implied that we were inferior. I never felt inferior, nor did I know anyone who felt inferior. My Army experiences may have paved the way for my later involvement in civil rights. A perennial discord sounded when I listened to elementary-school children singing 'My Country 'Tis of Thee.' This became a huge joke, given the disparity between the words of the song and the experiences of black men in the Army."

Another opportunity to gain a broader perspective occurred when his tour in the Army took him to India. "I traveled to India and lived in the midst of stench, pain, hunger, and death from September 1943 until July 1944," he recalls. As with most of his life's journey, he vividly remembers the time and the impact of the experience on him: "India gave me my first glimpse of what life must have been like during the time of Christ. People with no shoes and almost no clothes on, probably due to the climate, lived in little huts with dirt floors. People slept on the street. They bathed in tepid pools of water that had turned green from standing so long. There were no doctors. Illnesses that I had not heard of — malaria, elephantiasis, dysentery, leprosy, and typhoid fever — were rampant there. I saw mothers with little babies begging. India appeared to be a country of beggars. This is not to say that every person in India lived that way. Obviously they didn't. There was some semblance of a middle class, and there were maharajahs. However, you could hardly walk the street, especially in the big cities, without being approached time and time again by people begging.

"I wondered how people could enjoy life under such circumstances. I reconciled my wonder with the understanding that if this is all you have ever known, what else is there to enjoy?

"My trip to India brought about a realization of what it must have meant to live almost two thousand years ago, during the time of Christ. Other than that, the trip had no real effect upon me. However, I was disappointed with some of my fellow black soldiers, because they seemed to view the Indians as inferior and treated them as such. The nonchalant response that I would get when I talked to them about the similarities between the way they treated the people of India and the way white people treated Negroes in the South was troubling. I did come to the realization that there was no virtue in being black! I concluded that black people acted like white people when they had the power."

He does recall one life-transforming experience that occurred in India. Again, his life was saved: "While I was in the Army, stationed in Jorhat, Assam, India, I was working under a two-ton truck when someone, unaware of my presence, got in the truck and drove away. Debris spewed into my face as the deafening noise of the engine sounded in my ears. My main concern was protecting my head from being struck and crushed by the low underpinnings of the truck. I attempted to double my body up, but that did not stop the rapidly moving vehicle from running over my legs. I was taken to the field dispensary and later walked away completely unscathed."

When asked his religion during those years in the military service, he proudly announced, "I am Apostolic." In retrospect, he realizes that the words held no particular power or meaning for him. They represented rote recitation of something he had inherited and were completely without experiential knowledge of what in religious terms is called "putting on the new man." As he muses, he stops to recite a passage of Scripture: "… if any man be in Christ, he is a new creature: old things are passed away; behold, all things are become new."

Even though he seemed to be "spiritually dead" when he was discharged from the United States Army on December 28, 1945 (he had been drafted on October 26, 1942, it seems that he was being directed toward a definite path. At the time, unknown to him, he was being guided to the path of salvation.

In January 1946 he went to the state employment office to apply for a job. He recalls, "The person at the desk asked me how long I had been out of the Army. I told her I had been out two weeks. She expressed surprised that I was looking for a job so soon and asked me why I didn't sign up for a program called 5220 [a readjustment program that paid twenty dollars per week for fifty-two weeks]. I signed up and loafed around during January and February, waiting for the mailman to bring the check, but I realized that was not the kind of life that I was particularly happy with. Consequently, in 1946, when there was an opening, my friends who were working at Standard Steel

Corporation on the north side got me a job as a spot welder. I worked there for about a year and got a job at Western Electric for another year. In 1948 I was employed by the United States Postal Service. After twelve years I resigned to enter ministry full time."

After discharge from the Army, Brazier spent his days working and his nights continuing to enjoy the experiences of "being in the world." He was carousing and drinking Miller beer in Warner's Tavern at 33rd and Cottage Grove in Chicago one evening when someone called out, "Brazier, what religion are you?"

The response he uttered came from a place within him that he hadn't known before. "I am a sinner," is what bellowed forth from his innermost being. Something had prompted him to name the condition under which he lived. It was not long after this event in the tavern that he was saved.

"Being saved meant there was a real change in my life," he acknowledges. "From the very moment that I began to feel the need for Christ, my thought pattern began to change. The Bible began to take on more significance, although I did not understand it. The turning point came when I was reading from the twenty-first chapter of Revelation.

"It's amazing that one who is not a Bible scholar would read the book of Revelation, the last book in the world that most folks want to read because it is the hardest book to understand. However, I was reading from that twenty-first chapter, where the Scripture says, 'And I saw a new heaven and a new earth; for the first heaven and the first earth were passed away, and there was no more sea.' John continues to write, saying he 'heard a great voice out of heaven saying, "Behold: the tabernacle of God is with men, and he will dwell with them, and they shall be his people, and God himself shall be with them, and be their God."' He goes on to say, 'And God shall wipe away all tears from their eyes; and there shall be no more death, neither sorrow, nor crying, neither shall there be any more pain;

for former things are passed away.' And then the eighth verse, which says, 'But the fearful, and unbelieving, and the abominable ... and all liars, shall have their part in the lake which burneth with fire and brimstone, which is the second death.'"

The memory of the moment in which one is saved is etched on the soul. Forty-six years have passed since this event for Bishop Brazier, yet he recites these passages of Scripture as if he is being called at this moment by the Holy Spirit to know his presence and power. (Among Pentecostals the pronoun reference to the Holy Spirit is always masculine.)

Like his father, in some ways the Bishop is a laid-back man. Consequently, when he speaks, there is no doubt that he is often responding to something stirring deep within him. He says, "These verses sealed my determination to be saved. In fact, I was reading the Bible shortly before going to work. I was working the three-to-eleven shift at Western Electric. I told my father to go and get my mother, who happened to be in the kitchen, and to tell her that I wanted to be saved. He immediately got up and went to the kitchen and brought her back. I talked to my mother, and we prayed. She took me to church two or three days later."

Arthur Brazier was 26 when he was baptized at what is now the Apostolic Pentecostal Church of Morgan Park by Elder Sloan Woods. The church was pastored by Elder Herbert C. Moore, the uncle of his future wife, Esther Isabel Holmes.

He was 27 when he recognized his call to the ministry, within a few months of his being saved, but it took him several years to become comfortable with the fact that he was actually being called by God into ministry. He struggled to distinguish between being genuinely chosen by God and merely having a personal desire to help people in a humanitarian way which is associated with religion. This distinction was extremely important to him because of his belief "that preaching is a divine call, the most important undertaking a person can assume, and it should not be assumed on one's own initiative."

Bishop Brazier believes that without a true call and without the continuing aid of the Holy Spirit, the efforts of a person are fruitless. His initial response to what he recognized as the call of God was complicated by a feeling that preaching seemed to be beyond what he felt capable of doing. Though he could not name what he lacked, he could not easily dismiss the feeling.

He reports feeling depressed about the call. "I will never forget. I did not understand. I was working as a molder's helper at Western Electric's Archer Avenue plant. I had just been baptized, and I wished that the urge to preach would go away. It was something compelling. My main goal was to get a life-time job and take care of my family. The job I had set my sights on was with the United States Postal Service. When I was hired in 1948, I felt elated; I had never looked beyond this [goal]. Yet, at the same time, I had preached what seemed like a thousand sermons to the audience in my head. I was carried away by the words of Jesus, the apostles, and John the Baptist. My mental sermons were mostly focused on Christ taking away our sins, John baptizing Jesus, and the great miracles that Jesus performed."

The urge to preach remained. "There were some problems early on. At times I was very depressed about the call, and I really thought I would be happier if all I had to do was sit in the pew. This feeling was not [consistently present]. It would come and go. It lasted one to three hours, but it would come on a fairly regular basis. [This lasted] five to seven years, but it never overshadowed my desire to be a minister of God. It eventually left me. It ceased sometime after I became a pastor.

"I attended Moody Bible Institute at night [1955 to 1961] because I realized that I needed a greater understanding of the Bible in order to teach and preach. [His responsibilities for a job and a family did not allow for the option of full-time study.] I was seeking systematic Bible training. I viewed the Bible as the inspired Word of God, and it was important to me to not get caught up in denominationalism."

When God calls a man and he answers, various questions arise, questions like "What kind of a person should I be?" This seems like a simple question, but, like many other questions heard in the sermons, Bible study, and counseling sessions of Bishop Arthur Brazier, it subtly leads the questioner to contemplate the moral, ethical, emotional, social, and religious complexities required in living the life of a person who has been saved. This is a question that has had relevance for all humans since the beginning of time. The question implies that life is not predetermined, that to some extent a person plays a role in the development of his or her character.

How did Bishop Brazier come to see, to hear, and to think in ways that prepared him for the call and for "life under grace"? Were there markers, signs, that foretold what lay ahead for the man born Arthur Monroe Brazier?

In essence, one who is called and answers the call is empowered to help those who want to be transformed into new creatures through the love and labor of the called one. Rev. Henri Nouwen, author of The Wounded Healer, describes the role of the called one, the minister, as speaking to the ultimate concerns of life: birth and death, union and separation, love and hate. He sees the minister's call as one that recognizes both the suffering of his or her time and in his or her own heart. Coupling a concern for social justice with a spiritual concern, Bishop Brazier speaks to the ultimate concerns of "new creatures in Christ" because he is called by God to do so.

The called one, once anointed by the Holy Spirit, is the messenger who, as psychoanalyst Carl Jung says, is imbued with the skills of an alchemist, one who can change base metal into gold or, in psychological terms, can transform base human characteristics into the Creator's image of what the human ought to be as he or she struggles to claim the Creator's promise of being remade in the Creator's image. For Bishop Brazier, this radical change occurs when one encounters the transformative power of the Holy Spirit: "the Holy Spirit leads us; it helps us to recover ourselves when we have fallen short."

The alchemist/theologian seasons his or her transformation by the Holy Spirit and his or her interpretion of the Word with love. Harnessing the power of the Word and living in love, Bishop Brazier speaks to his people, interprets the Word, and struggles to live according to the gospel. He radiates God's love not just because he has answered God's call but also because he knows suffering intimately and has been anointed by God.

The called one is required to live in and to participate in the society of his or her time, not to withdraw and shield himself or herself from the sight of those whom Howard Thurman, theologian, philosopher, educator, and mystic, calls the disinherited or from the political and economic conditions that are prevalent in society. The call cannot be separated from what Brazilian multicultural educator Paulo Freire identifies as praxis. Critical reflection must be put into practice in collective action.

Theologians Jose Comblin and James Forbes note the animation of spirit that results when the called one sees a direct relationship between the Holy Spirit and the social-justice needs of minority people. Their ideas are exemplified in what Bishop Brazier has done, both in his congregation, regardless of its size, and in the community. He views the church as playing a vital role in teaching and preaching about the Holy Spirit, the power of the Word of God, the meaning of the Word of God, and the manifestation of the Spirit in the lives of the people for whom he has been called to preach the Word of the God of the gospel. The seeds for the development of the kind of action described here are often planted within one's family of origin. However, the roots really take hold when a person is called and answers the call. The roots are nurtured when the called one embraces what Robert Greenleaf and Morton Kelsey describe as the life of servant leadership, which has a dual focus: caring for and learning to love self and others.

Is the person who is called first prepared to be the human vessel that will contain, process, and then speak the Word of God, or is the person simply given the message regardless of his or her transformation and readiness? There are indicators that Bishop Brazier falls into the first category. He speaks of "something being born" in him, something he could not articulate but something that led him to delay making decisions until he had a clear sense that what he wanted to do was not his will but the will of the Holy Spirit. Throughout his life he recalls feeling that God had "his hand on him."

It is difficult for Bishop Brazier to describe this experience. He searches for words that can be both spoken by him and understood by another and finally says, "I think that one can only really talk about God having his hand on you when you look back. This is not something that one can say is happening at any particular point and time in the present. I think that one has to look back and see the path that has been traveled and how things occurred in life, things that normally, if the decision had been solely left up to you, you would have taken a different direction. Say, for instance, God spared your life. You cannot answer the question of why you were spared when others died until you understand your purpose.

"Life experiences are not random but are tied to the individual's journey. Many experiences seem to be intended to prepare you for the work you are to do. For example, in my case, what was it that God had for me that sent me to

India instead of England and France? What happened to me that made me feel a need and a desire to be saved? Being saved meant there was a real change in my life, and from the very moment that I began to feel the need for Christ in my life, my thought pattern began to change. The Bible began to take on more significance, although I did not understand it. No, one can only retrospectively or with evidence speak of God's hand being on him or her."

5

After the Call

Also I heard the voice of the Lord, saying,
Whom shall I send, and who will go for us?
Then said I, Here am I; send me.
                                        — Isaiah 6:8

What characterizes life under grace? [We]
testify that [we] are saved. What kind of life
should [we] live? God sees [us] in [our]
private lives.
                                        — Arthur M. Brazier

After Bishop Brazier became a pastor, he felt depressed. He
describes his emotional state as "having moods." "Serious
anxiety swings" would envelop him as each Sunday
neared. The dialogue in his head sounded like a tape that
played a familiar refrain: "Will I have something to say?
Will I say it so the people of God will be strengthened?"

The theologian Karl Barth writes about the role of this
kind of doubt in the life of one who has been called. He
suggests that doubt is part and parcel of the theological
quest for truth. This is a quest that is never completed, one
that engages the theologian throughout life. Barth contends
that not everyone is prepared for the level of repeated self-
exposure demanded of one who follows this path.

Bishop Brazier agrees with Barth and reveals that even
today, after years of preaching, there remain vestiges of
doubt. "I wonder when I stand before the people, will I

have something meaningful to say to them?" he confesses.

When pressed, Bishop Brazier acknowledges that an awareness of his being anointed and guided by the Holy Spirit causes the doubt to leave as quickly as it came, because the question "Is there any word from the Lord?" brings the immediate response that there is always word from the Lord. The called one needs only to still him- or herself in order to hear the message.

Bishop Brazier is also concerned about arousing people's emotions either through music or through preaching. (The power of the music ministry of the Apostolic Church of God has earned the choir the honor of performing in prestigious places such as Chicago's Orchestra Hall.) He frequently reminds the congregation that "feeling and rejoicing in the Spirit," no matter where one is, is not the same as "emotionalism."

"[Emotionalism is] superficial. It makes [the hearer] feel good, but it is not what is needed in the time of testing and temptation," he says. He views emotionalism as something that passes, and when it does, people need the depth of their being touched in order to be sustained. He believes that "only the exaltation of Jesus" will give one such lasting results.

Bishop Brazier feels that the demands of his call are as relevant today as they were some forty-six years ago. They are directly related to his continuing effort to deepen his understanding of the Word, to modify his actions accordingly, and to lead his congregants on a similar quest. He believes that it is through guidance from the Holy Spirit that he has been led to examine and to separate tradition (which often results in indoctrinating people) from what is actually written in Scripture.

"Too often, instead of Scripture, tradition-governed customs or values prescribe behavior, for example, women wearing open-toed shoes, makeup, and jewelry; families going to ball games or watching television," Bishop Brazier says. While religion is intended to instill pervasive basic values that remain throughout one's life, the saved person is not expected to deny what it means to be born in the flesh. The challenge is no less today than it was ages ago when Saint Paul wrote of his struggle: 'For the good that I would, I do not; but the evil which I would not, that I do.'

"Being in tune with the Holy Spirit is the way to avoid being trapped by the physical. At the same time one needs to be respectful of the power that is wielded in the physical realm. Avoidance of either extreme is crucial. Neither leads to a life that allows the person to seek the promise of God for his or her life. The excessive prohibition of pleasure too often leads to people turning away from the church and falling prey to a life of unbridled pleasure."

After his call, a religious perspective began to affect everything that Bishop Brazier did. He lived out of a religious core. In this respect he resembles the late Dr. Martin Luther King Jr., for whom, according to Howard Thurman, the center his "personal religious experience" was a search for ethical awareness and an understanding of his Judeo-Christian heritage.

Those around Bishop Brazier sense a similar serious and devout religious intentionality in the Bishop, and they speak about it. In one situation Susan Smith, a pharmacist and the wife of Dr. Horace Smith, the pastor of the Apostolic Faith Church, rose from her seat at a conference when someone was speaking in what appeared to be an unconsciously negative way about Bishop Brazier. She announced, as she got to her feet and departed from the room, "I love my Bishop, and I will not be a party to a discussion that misinterprets his message." Those who were engaged in the discussion appeared to harbor no ill will, yet their comments could be interpreted as implying a self-serving spirit in the Bishop. They were sharing their versions of the early days of the church and in the process making jokes about how Bishop Brazier managed money and people. Mrs. Smith's defense of the Bishop demonstrates how she, and other people, judge him to be a model of integrity and spirituality.

On another occasion, Patti Caire, commenting on Bishop Brazier, said, "The rest of us make decisions about what we think God wants us to do. Bishop waits for word from the Lord no matter how long it takes. That's why he has been so successful."

The requirement to live in the tension between the spiritual and the temporal realms can be clearly seen and heard in Bishop Brazier's references to and interactions with his family. He describes himself as a man who loves his family. They are second only to the call on his life; they are central to his perception of what grounds him as a man.

Esther Isabel Holmes, who became Bishop Brazier's wife, was born March 24, 1929, in Indianapolis. She met Arthur M. Brazier when she was 18 and he was 26. She had come to Chicago from Indianapolis to pursue a career in interior design because there were few opportunities for blacks in her hometown. The two of them met at a church picnic that Bishop Brazier was attending at his mother's request. When he agreed to go, he added, "If I go, I am going to look for a wife."

Esther Brazier observes, "He [Bishop Brazier] thought that his mother would say, 'Son, if that is what you are going for, you don't need to go.' Instead she said, 'Sure, come on.' This happened in July 1947."

A wife was indeed what he found.

Esther Holmes was baptized at age 10 and "received the Holy Ghost at age 15." (The two spiritual events do not very often occur simultaneously. One can be baptized and never experience an "infilling of the Holy Spirit.") She was active in the church. She recalls that Bishop Brazier was not saved at the time of the picnic, "but the Lord was dealing with him all the time."

"In September 1947 he received the Holy Ghost," she says. We were engaged in October. I went back to

Indianapolis, and he commuted on weekends. By February he asked to move up the date of the wedding. A sticking point was housing, which was at a premium in the late forties, but I had never lived in an apartment. Therefore, I refused to marry him until he found a house."

She finally relented and agreed to marry despite not having a house; instead, they rented a large room in the home of Elder Ahart Medders, then the assistant pastor of the Apostolic Church of God. The temporary room lasted through four years and two babies. Even in this living arrangement she sees God's hand in their lives. It provided fertile ground for the seed of ministry to germinate. She recalls, "The call came six months before he told me. I suspected he had been called because of his behavior. He was involved in rigorous studying and engaging in lengthy discussion with Elder Walter M. Clemons."

During this time Bishop Brazier also spent Tuesday and Thursday evenings and all day on Sundays at his mother's church and Wednesday and Friday evenings at the Apostolic Church of God, Elder Clemons's church.

The Braziers today have four children — Lola, Byron, Janice, and Rosalyn — born respectively on March 26, 1949; March 26, 1950; February 8, 1955; and August 30, 1956. "They grew up in church similar to the way I did," Bishop Brazier says. "I was very fortunate because they never left the church as I did. When Lola was young, she would go with me on preaching assignments. She would sit on the front pew. Her legs were so short they could not reach the floor. My children were normal children. They got into trouble, but they never gave us any serious difficulties. They did not assume a lot of the bad habits of some of their peers, like smoking, drinking, and experimenting with drugs. They eventually became active members in the church and dedicated their lives to the Lord. My son, Byron, after being a Sunday-school teacher for twenty years, informed me Christmas Day 1992 that he felt a call to the ministry."

Bishop Brazier is obviously pleased that his children's own paths have not taken them away from him or the church.

Mrs. Brazier remained home until 1965, when her youngest child was 9. She then felt a need for additional dimensions to her life and for developing her own talent more fully. "I felt like an individual who needed to explore my dreams," she says. "I wanted an identity of my own."

She became an active volunteer at the children's schools and at church while her husband was in school besides working full-time and pastoring a struggling church. She recalls that the struggle meant "he would often pay the church's debt out of the money he earned. Back in those days the ministry was a low-paying job. I felt I had to do something because I thought my husband would be a struggling preacher for good. However, God blessed us beyond my wildest dreams.

"Times [financially] got very difficult. We moved from a three-room eighty-seven-dollar-a-month apartment into a three-bedroom hundred-and-fifty-dollar-a-month apartment in the first high rise in Lake Meadows [a middle-income housing development] before the building was completed. We did not have money to buy a house."

By this time Mrs. Brazier had given up her dream of becoming an interior designer because of financial and family pressures. (She had studied briefly at the Vogue School of Design in Chicago.) When the family pressures eased, the financial pressures continued, and she began to think about employment. One obstacle to her working, however, was her husband's objection. Bishop Brazier's objection was based upon the belief that a "man should be able to provide for his family." Although his mother periodically worked by taking in "washing," his father had always been the primary breadwinner.

"I suppose that my reason for not wanting my wife to work was based on false pride," he says. "In fact, my wife and I never merged our incomes. I never asked her to pay any household bills of any kind. Nor did I ever ask her how much she made, and I tried to act as if she were not working at all. There was no question, however, that her additional income gave great financial aid to the family. Without conferring with me, she purchased food and assisted in buying clothes for the children. Had it not been for my false pride, we may have gotten a lot farther a lot faster!

"I don't know where this attitude came from, but one thing I know is that I didn't want her to work. I felt that was my role. This was embedded in my mind. Maybe it had its origin in the fact that my mother never left home at say eight o'clock and returned at five o'clock. She worked mostly at home. She washed and ironed the clothes there, and my cousin Walter, who had a car, would take them to the people she worked for. Twice a week she would go to their homes, but not every day. Of course, my father was gone every day.

"My wife felt like we were not making it. She really bothered me until finally I said, 'If you want to go to work, go ahead!' When I look back on it now, my way was not the best way. However, at the time my position on the issue gave the illusion that I was taking care of my family. Sometimes pride does not let you do the wisest thing."

The agreement came after a "spirited discussion" in which Mrs. Brazier is reported to have convinced her husband that his income was not adequate to take care of a family of six.

Mrs. Brazier was employed in direct services and personnel administration for fourteen years at Planned Parenthood. She left that position in 1979 because of organizational downsizing. By this time the growth of the church had increased the need for her to spend time on church projects that were very important to her, such as developing programs for the youth.

A look at a pastor's wife always raises the question "When God calls a man, is his wife also primed to assume the role she is called upon to play?" Bishop Brazier believes that "when God calls a man to pastor, his wife is given patience and an innate understanding of the role. These two characteristics are especially important because the wife of a pastor has more influence on him than any other individual does. Yet she must try to understand that she should not substitute her judgment for that of the pastor. Often a wife can feel that her input is of no value merely because it is not followed. What a pastor is looking for from his wife is sometimes not so much counseling or advice, but support. Frequently, when he has already made up his mind, his wife may feel a sense of rejection if her advice was not followed.

According to Bishop Brazier, "The pastor is the leader of the congregation, and much of the success of the congregation will depend upon his leadership. However, honesty and forthrightness are important. One must keep in mind that the advice given [by a pastor's wife] is advice and advice only!" Although the question under consideration here is the place of a pastor's wife, Bishop Brazier states that the same situation can also be a challenge for husbands of clergywomen.

It seems in this union that both persons have answered their particular call — Bishop Brazier as pastor and Mrs. Brazier as the wife of the pastor who is also a bishop. Bishop Brazier is quick to say that although he is the official head of his household, he has remained aware of the presence and the influence of his wife. Adds Mrs. Brazier, "Although I have a special relationship with my husband, he is the one with the 'special' relationship with God. As a wife, sometimes I plant seeds that influence my husband. However, I am not concerned about running the church; I am concerned about him."

The Anointing
of the Messenger

6

Preparation of the Practical Theologian

*The Spirit of the Lord is upon me, because he
hath anointed me to preach the gospel to the
poor; he hath sent me to heal the
brokenhearted, to preach deliverance to the
captives, and recovering of sight to the blind,
to set at liberty them that are bruised.*

— *Luke 4:18*

*God chose [me], called [me], guided [me] ....
Not just to care for the scarred souls of the
people .... Often the scars caused by social
injustice must be attended to before the
preacher can reach the [heaven-bound] souls
of the people.*

— *Arthur M. Brazier*

Bishop Arthur M. Brazier's twofold spiritual endeavors are
preaching the Word as inspired through the presence of
the Holy Spirit and living a life that exemplifies what he
preaches (that Jesus Christ died that we might live, that
our sins are forgiven, that new birth changes our lives,
and that eternal security comes as a result of being saved
by Jesus Christ). Preaching, teaching, and serving as a
social-justice advocate (one who champions the rights of
others to participate equally in society) are the primary
imperatives of the call Bishop Brazier received. He
considers himself to be a practical theologian whose

thinking is focused on action rather than on general theory. His particular bent as a social-justice advocate is illustrated in his book *Black Self-Determination* and in his long involvement with civil rights (affordable housing, community development, and school desegregation).

Bishop Brazier's involvement in social justice, or civil rights, was a "baptism by fire," but certain of these experiences led to the preparation of the anointed one. He recalls three major challenges: "I really became involved in civil rights in 1960, when I met Saul Alinsky [well-known community organizer and director of the Industrial Areas Foundation (IAF)]. He persuaded me to become active in organizing what is now called the Woodlawn Organization. It was formed in 1961," the Bishop says.

Bishop Brazier played a major role in the movement to organize the Woodlawn Organization to stabilize living, social, and economic conditions in this south-Chicago community. As with many of the political and social movements in the black community, the Woodlawn Organization was given life by the church.

According to Bishop Brazier, the organization was created as a response to four deeply committed pastors in the community who were concerned about eroding housing, crime, unemployment, and the lack of quality education for the children of Woodlawn. Their conversation continually came back to the inescapable conclusion that within two to three years Woodlawn would become a major slum unless a vigorous community organization was developed to stem the deterioration that was spreading across the neighborhood.

Brazier and the other pastors represented an ecumenically and racially inclusive group that formed an alliance in which the central focus was on developing indigenous leaders. The group was adamant that leadership be appointed from within the community and not be imposed by those outside the community. The alliance felt it was imperative that black men learn that they do not have to rely upon leadership appointed by the white power structure.

TWO (the Woodlawn Organization) was a cooperative venture that included civic, religious, and other community organizations committed to working on the improvement and the enrichment of life in an urban society·in areas such as housing, education, health, employment, and government. The organization's basic philosophy was to develop standards and values for community living and to work for a well-ordered society that would show concern for the welfare of all the people, without regard to race, color, religious creed, national origin, or social station.

The Woodlawn alliance decided to engage the services of IAF to help the community organize. This decision was supported because the IAF had a philosophy that matched the community's, i.e., that tactics and principles must arise out of and be articulated by the specific society and community in which they were to be worked out.

During the organizing period, Nicholas Von Hoffman, chief organizer of IAF, and his staff took positions within the community. Bishop Brazier assumed the role of official spokesman for TWO, and Rev. Robert J. McGee, assistant pastor of the Apostolic Church of God, was elected temporary president.

"At that time the University of Chicago was making serious effort to expand its campus into Woodlawn," Bishop Brazier explains. The university's campus stopped at the Midway Plaisance [60th Street]. They wanted to move from 60th to 61st Street [southern boundary] and from Cottage Grove [western boundary] to Stony Island [eastern boundary]. Obviously there was going to be displacement, which was labeled by the black community not as urban renewal but as Negro removal.

"Many of the people who lived in Woodlawn had been

victims of the urban-renewal program that took place when Lake Meadows, a housing project developed by New York Life Insurance Company, was built. Lake Meadows stretched from Lake Park Avenue to South Park [renamed Martin Luther King Drive] and from 31st Street to 35th Street.

"I was raised in the [Lake Meadows] area. During the time I was in the Army, housing in the area was allowed to become dilapidated because of the plan to raze it and develop the new housing project.

"There was an uproar in Woodlawn, and one of the issues that TWO organized around was preventing the university from further expanding into Woodlawn. The struggle was finally settled when the community agreed that the university could move one block, from 60th to 61st Street.

"In 1963 the sting was taken out of this expansion when the city, in turn, agreed to tear down dilapidated business structures on Cottage Grove on both sides of the street from 61st to 63rd and to build new low-income housing called 221D3 housing. The subsidized housing units were constructed under the Federal Housing Act.

"The next major challenge was the gang wars. I was president of TWO [1964], and people in the community were asking what the organization could do about the gangs. In 1965 and 1966 the gang war was at full-blown strength. There was a war between the Blackstone Rangers and the East Side Disciples. It was basically a turf war. As far as I know, there were no drugs involved, but there was a lot of shooting. Families in Woodlawn could not send their children to school because of the gang problems. Consequently, several members of TWO tried to find ways to address the problem. We had discussions with representatives from several large corporations in an effort to identify resources for the community. I was given the name of Jerry Bernstein, director of the Office of Economic Opportunity [OEO], as a possible funding contact.

"In 1966 I approached Bernstein while attending a civil-rights conference called by President Lyndon B. Johnson in Washington, D.C. He asked me to send him an abstract of the program we wanted to develop. The proposal was funded by OEO for $927,000. The Woodlawn Organization set up four community-based training centers — two for the Blackstone Rangers and two for the East Side Disciples. This structure was necessary because the tension between the two gangs was such that they could not function together.

"The training program gave a twenty-five-dollar-a-week stipend to the participants. They also were given physical, dental, and eye examinations and transportation costs if they lived too far to walk to the centers.

"The funding for the training centers was awarded to TWO. We knew that the program was going to be under attack. Therefore, we hired a prestigious accounting firm to set up the financial system, to monitor it every thirty days, and to provide us with an annual audit.

"TWO's receipt of the funding created serious turmoil in Chicago because there were a number of people who were against the project. The program was seriously impeded by obstructionists. The police department was never in favor of it. In fact, I met several times with the superintendent of police, O.W. Wilson, whom I considered to be a fine man, but he always referred to the gang members as criminals. At that time I did not see the youths in the gangs as criminals. I saw them as misguided youths who were forming gangs out of some false conception that this was something they needed. Therefore, there was a lot of harassing from the police department. They would walk into the centers unannounced; they would take people out.

"The most unfortunate incident occurred because of allegations that the gang leaders were misusing the funds. Checks that were issued to legitimate participants were forged by some of the gang leaders. As a result of this we went through three major investigations conducted by the Office of Economic Opportunity, the General Accounting

Office of the United States, and the United States Senate. In spite of the financial monitoring system, funds were still misused. The same handwriting was used to forge the names on all of the checks. It was like anything else: where there is a will, there is a way. However, I faulted the accounting firm for this failure. How could this occur when they were monitoring every thirty days? This should have been caught and brought to our attention.

"I discovered the forged endorsements when federal agents walked into my office and gave me a subpoena demanding that I turn over the records. I refused; they left and came back with a list of certain records. I told them that I would give them copies. This was the day before the Fourth of July. My secretary and I spent the Fourth of July copying the fronts and backs of checks. The federal agents returned in a month and asked for the originals. In December 1968 they subpoenaed everything. I bundled up everything and called the accounting firm to send a truck to pick up the records. I did not want to leave records in the event someone broke in. The records remained there until after the trial."

When asked about his present perspective on this event, Bishop Brazier says, "I think the idea was a good one. I still think that the youths who were in the project at the time were misguided. Obviously the shooting and killing were terrible. We focused on trying to stop the violence and to win one person or two people out of the gang structure, which was almost impossible. We tried to turn the whole structure around with something that was beneficial rather than destructive.

"Initially I was under the impression that we had received the support of the power structure in this city. I was wrong. We did not. I know that the police department was not supportive. It turned out that neither were the [community] schools. They continually said that our program was enticing young people to drop out of school so they could get the twenty-five-dollar stipends. So, in response to this, we set rules that said a participant had to be out of school for six months before he or she could join the program. There was one thing after another; plus, the gangs never stopped shooting. I think our biggest mistakes were being too optimistic and not having a larger professional staff.

"We contracted with the Xerox Corporation to develop the educational materials. The man assigned to the project moved his family to Chicago while he set up the educational system. We really had a good system in place. However, we only had three staff persons, and we were depending upon gang leaders to keep control of the youths in these centers. We needed at least five staff persons for each center. Perhaps in the fifth year we could have reduced the staff from twenty to five or six. We were also hampered by never being able to hire a permanent director, because one of the special conditions of the grant was that the mayor of the city of Chicago had to concur with our choice of a director. The two sides, TWO and the mayor, could never reach a mutual decision on who should be the director. I finally hired a person; however, he was not a qualified social worker.

"We hired Irving Spergel from the University of Chicago (we had confidence in him because of the national reputation of his work with gangs) to write an objective evaluation on the project. It was a lengthy document which recommended that the project continue. It did not, and we were required to return approximately $300,000 to the federal government."

The third challenge confronting Bishop Brazier during the sixties was connected to school and housing segregation. He says, "It was the housing segregation that brought Dr. Martin Luther King to Chicago. This is how I became involved with him. It was during the demonstrations against segregated housing that I received harassing telephone calls that included serious threats against my life, not from the gangs but from the people who were involved in housing segregation. I was informed by the police department that the threats should be taken seriously. Consequently, for several weeks bodyguards were assigned to me from the time I left home until I returned. Once someone also called in a threat to bomb the church. None of this, however, deterred the members of the congregation nor myself."

The creation and maintenance of economically integrated African American communities have remained an important thrust of Bishop Brazier's social-justice interest. This idea of an economically integrated community grows out of a time past when this was the only option for most black people, and it worked. Due to segregation there was no real social-class stratification in the community; for example, physicians, mail carriers, social workers, factory workers, and welfare recipients all lived fairly harmoniously in the same community.

7

Anointing of the Messenger

The call marks the beginning of the life-long
studying required to prepare one to preach
the gospel to the people of God.
— *Arthur M. Brazier*

The anointing of the messenger returns us to the question of the preparation of the messenger, of the process, of the deepening that is necessary for one to live out the role of messenger of the God of the gospel. Does the call itself significantly change or prepare the person for the work? Is the person changed through carrying out the work? Is a theological education the enabler? Or is there yet another, more mysterious, operative element?

The studies in theological education edited by Don Browning, David Polk, and Ian Evison, along with the works of Jose Comblin, James Forbes, Henri Nouwen, and Paul Tillich, seem to imply that the called one is shaped by various experiences. Each of these writers focuses on a particular formative influence, i.e., theological education, practical theology, preaching the Word, and social justice, though sometimes their ideas about formative influences overlap.

For Bishop Brazier the dichotomy between practice and theory is a false one. He sees no practical utility in theological pontificating. For him, the confirmation of one's anointing is apparent not in eloquently spoken words but in the called one's calling the church into physical and financial partnership with social organizations with the result that the disinherited can find a place of refuge.

Bishop Brazier believes that "[we] should keep a watchful eye on philosophical meanderings that take us away from Christ." This admonition includes the reminder that Scripture is not to be violated in the blending of the theological, the philosophical, and the practical. He also sees the depth and breadth of a call unfolding as the called one participates in preparation, reflection, and service. However, Bishop Brazier is convinced that such deepening and growth are not so much anticipated at the time as recognized by hindsight, later in life. He believes that "through the periodic reflecting on or looking backward over one's life it is revealed whether the guiding force has been the Holy Sirit or some other voice."

Reflecting upon the nature of the practical theologian in his book The Education of the Practical Theologian, Peter J. Paris identifies the personal character of the called one as an important aspect of being a practical theologian. He believes that moral and religious sensibility cannot be overestimated. They are central to personal conviction, which, he contends, is not determined by the development of the intellect in abstract from the character of the person.

Paris further warns that the absence of a certain type of character is perilous to the goals of what he calls effective moral and religious training. Paris makes it clear that he does not see theological education in and of itself as capable of changing the moral disposition or religious convictions of a person. The type of character needed in the practical theologian is exemplified by Bishop Brazier's searching questions: "What kind of person should I be?" and "What characterizes life under grace?"

Paris's focus is not only on the character of the individual but also on his or her concern for and involvement in the eradication of the major moral problems of contemporary society, for example, apartheid, economic deprivation, women's issues, war and peace, racism, governmental responsibility for the well-being of the citizens, and a host of others.

Though Bishop Brazier clearly places significance on all forms of education, like Paris, he considers the called one's character to be of greater value than education. He says, "God uses people where they are. One's educational level does not determine one's role in carrying out God's plan. However, ongoing preparation must occur regardless of whether one has a third-grade or a seminary education."

It seems that preparation includes the call, the development of the character of the person, a theological education, and a bent for social justice. As Bishop Brazier says, "The wedding of these elements through the anointing of the Holy Spirit is what prepares the vessel to issue forth its contents in such a way that others are changed by their encounter with it. The Holy Spirit continuously provides that which is necessary to transform the vessel as it participates in the transformation of those who come to it seeking the living Word of the God of the gospel." Jose Comblin echoes this line of thinking when he says that an experience with the Holy Spirit is the kind of experience that can lead to the true God. He further argues that only those who have an experience with the Holy Spirit are able to read the Gospels and speak of the true Jesus Christ. Those who rely upon their understanding alone or on "their literary and historical knowledge" are seen by Comblin as not being able to approach "the real Christ who is alive today."

Bishop Brazier's insistence upon "following the Scripture and not the tradition and [upon] waiting for Word from the Lord" before trudging into unchartered spiritual, physical, or emotional terrain is characteristic of a man who is growing in his knowledge of the Lord, of his individual purpose, and of the purpose of the church he serves — a man who has benefited from integrating the theological and practical aspects of the call.

In spite of Bishop Brazier's refusal to claim identity exclusively with either the intellectuals or the theologians, he is interested in the philosophical questions they pose. His anointment seems to call him to go beyond the questions and to challenge and lead people to change.

James Forbes points out that the prophet Ezekiel is an early example of what the ministry of an anointed one is like. Ezekiel was called to a ministry of helping those who were in exile experience a "sense of the land." Forbes describes him as one who was anointed and called to preach to people who had "been broken and made dead," people who felt separated from their spiritual center. Called and anointed, Ezekiel gave them hope in the midst of their hopelessness.

When Bishop Brazier speaks of his doubt about knowing whether or not he will have anything to say to the people, Forbes's words will assure him that he will have if he is anointed. For Forbes, preaching under the anointing is done always with the recognition that one does not know what to say unless he or she is told by the Lord. The Holy Spirit provides the person with words beyond what the person struggles to put together.

The improvement and the empowerment of preaching stems from reconnecting with and reclaiming the power and the presence of the Holy Spirit. Forbes describes himself as a "Tillichian Pentecostal," proclaiming the gospel with a curious combination of heart and head. He sees the Pentecostal emphasis on the experience of the Spirit as key to the tension between the "old-time religion" and the "new-age perspectives." Like Karl Barth and Bishop Brazier, Forbes emphasizes the importance of the connection between the lessons of the ancients and those of contemporaries.

Forbes characterizes his own style of ministry as "progressive Pentecostalism" — a strong emphasis on spirit with a deep commitment to transformative social action. Progressive Pentecostalism is also descriptive of the ministry Bishop Brazier carries out. Bishop Brazier's preparation after his anointing was however, somewhat different from the traditional path of preparation. However, the essential elements of reliance on guidance from the Holy Sirit (sometimes even unconscious reliance) and commitment to transformative social action can be seen over the span of his life.

Bishop Brazier contends that "the readiness which occurs when one prepares [to undertake ministry as an anointed on] still must be tempered with guidance from the Spirit. It includes time to seek clarity about the mission given to the person, time to determine the manner in which the mission is to be carried out, and time to discover the guidance which will determine how and by whom the work will be done."

Ultimately, Bishop Brazier sees the purpose of the anointing as leading to the mature sense of what a Christian really is — "One who integrates faith in every aspect of life." The experience of anointing, which is influenced by the Holy Spirit, is not primarily for the personal use of the called one, but for the anointed one to become a servant of God.

Recognizing that all Christians have the need for and the right to some theological education, some reflective practice, Bishop Brazier uses his position as a minister to teach as well as to preach, but he is convinced that the result of understanding the faith should be the practicing of the faith. To this end, Bishop Brazier's sermons are delivered at a level that allows the congregation to experience an encounter with the Word of God. He moves among the people and invites them, when possible, to engage in dialogue, through which he shares with them the Scriptures upon which their faith is built. (The size of the audiences makes this a formidable challenge.)

Bishop Brazier's own study methods, under the guidance of the Holy Spirit, are shared with the congregation. The dialogical quality of his sermons, Bible-study classes, FOCUS (Fostering Our Christian Unity and Strength) education series, congregational-care programs (married couples and singles groups, counseling and referral services), and forums in which the congregation has an opportunity to "ask the Bishop/pastor" demonstrate that his emphasis is on providing theological education for the congregation. In a more formal sense, he has taught seminarians at North Park Seminary in a course titled Churches' Involvement in Community Organization. Whether he is teaching inside the church or in the community, the liaison between knowing the faith and living the faith and between the church and the community is ever present in his message.

The intellectual, the philosopher, the theologian, and the social-justice activist all are combined to make up Arthur Brazier. Mostly he seems oblivious to the many dimensions he brings to ministry. When he is labeled, he is caught by surprise. He does not seem to hear himself or the Spirit moving in and through him when he quotes Aristotle, John Paul Sartre, Albert Camus, and a host of other, when he enriches his sermons with poetry, or when he shares a significant anecdote that makes the sermon more understandable to those who have not had the opportunity or the inclination to study and ponder the great philosophical or theological questions that arise once one has moved beyond living merely for material good.

Bishop Brazier does not view himself as an intellectual or a theologian. He is mindful of the intellectual traps into which people fall and of how one can become mesmerized by the charms and persuasivenss of language. His goal is to remain focused on preaching and teaching the message he has been given. He sees himself as having no real background in philosophy but as having a love of wisdom and knowledge and above all a love for God's Word and God's people. The avid reading, studying, reflecting, and social action he has engaged in throughout his life come together without conscious effort on his part. Yet, when viewed by another, even a detractor who vehemently disagrees with his doctrinal position, he stands out as a man of God who stands out among men.

Preparation of the Intellectual

*The anointing is the special presence of the
Holy Spirit ....*

> — *James Forbes*

*When we talk about becoming an
intellectual, ... we are really talking about
what it is to sit with one's ideas ....*

> — *bell hooks*

Bell hooks (she writes her name with all lower-case
letters) and Cornell West, in their book *Breaking Bread:
Insurgent Black Intellectual Life,* engage in a dialogue that
explores many aspects of black intellectual life. Hooks
asserts that when one speaks of becoming an intellectual
in the real, "life-enhancing" sense of the word, one is
really talking about what it means to sit with one's ideas.
She sees this process as using the mind as a workplace
where time is allotted for contemplation and critical
reflection on things. Hooks calls this experience
aloneness. For her it is time she spends listening to the
inner voice of God as it speaks to her in what she calls the
stillness of her life.

The seed for being comfortable with aloneness and
stillness were sown by Robert Brazier in his young son
Arthur, who sat on his father's lap or close by, mimicking
his father's stillness as he sat reading. The effect of his
father's practice of quiet reading can still be seen in the

son's acts of aloneness and stillness. Bishop Brazier can be found during even small snatches of time on any given day reading either at his desk or at the conference table in his office. In the evenings a strategically placed chair allows him to look out over the Chicago skyline and Lake Michigan as he reads, contemplates sermons, and ponders the Word of the Lord.

Bell hooks compares this kind of intellectual activity to Christ's going into the desert to find a place for renewal and spiritual enlightenment. She sees a similarity between aloneness and subsequently being able to more fully reenter community, and critical reflection and subsequent collective action. Hooks makes it clear that, although some aloneness is necessary, sharing in the renewal of the life of the community is equally necessary.

Cornell West makes a distinction between an "academic" and an "intellectual." He defines an academic as one who usually engages in rather important yet "narrow scholarly work," whereas an intellectual is one who engages in the public issues that affect large numbers of people in a critical way. By these definitions, Bishop Brazier is more an intellectual than an academic.

As a philosopher, the Bishop is mostly self-trained. Yet he has what West sees as the philosopher's fundamental concern with confronting death, dread, despair, disappointment, disease, and the inevitable doom that other intellectuals (sociologists, social scientists, and economists) may not have. He is concerned about issues that impact upon the whole person in the spiritual, intellectual, psychological, political, and economic realms. He does not hide behind the excuse that his position makes it necessary for him to be removed from the "worldly" concerns of those to whom he is called to preach the gospel. He enters the fray dressed in the "full armor of God" and with intellectual and philosophical perspectives that will enable him to bring together the community's understanding of its Christianity and its social responsibilities.

Inclusiveness is a primary outcome of his effort: "whosoever will" is invited to participate in fellowship with the church. The congregation is encouraged to explore the reality, the importance, and the impact of the political arena on the spiritual, social, and economic life of the congregation.

Antonio Gramsci, a political writer, sees all people as being potential intellectuals in the sense of having an intellect and using it, but he goes on to classify intellectuals into two groups: the "traditional" intellectuals, who represent fields like literature, science, economics, and so on, and the "organic" intellectuals, who are distinguished not by their professions but by their function in directing the ideas and aspirations of whatever group they belong to. Bishop Brazier, though he speaks and reads French fluently; has an acquaintance with the Greek language through his studies of Wuest's *Word Studies in the Greek New Testament,* Vincent's *Word Studies in the New Testament,* and Vine's *Expository Dictionary of Old and New Testament Words;* has also read many of the classics and other literature; and studies the interpretations of seven different Bibles when he is preparing a sermon or Bible-study lesson, still falls into the category of organic, not traditional, intellectual. As a preacher, he has little time or inclination for the ivory-tower activities of a traditional intellectual. His strength is to give ideas to the class to which he belongs: black urban leaders and preachers.

In the final analysis, Bishop Brazier seems to view labels such as "intellectual" as much ado about nothing. While he has tremendous respect for education, he also says that "the Holy Spirit works with people where they are. He [Holy Spirit] does not refuse to call, anoint, and prepare people [simply] because they are not charismatic speakers or credentialed by universities. The Spirit has work for all levels of preachers. He does not see the person who serves God as [being] either a dull or [a] sharp instrument. There are those who have not learned to read volumes of books, but God can still use them."

However, Bishop Brazier does see study and preparation as activities that increase the quality of service a person is able to render. They have helped move him from house church to storefront to cathedral after the call and the anointing had set him on the path of becoming a servant of God.

Arthur and Esther Brazier.

The Apostolic Church of God in Chicago (Left, lobby; right, main sanctuary).

Bishop Brazier and ministers sit in at Inland Steel in Chicago, 1963.

Ministers demonstrating against school desegregation in Chicago, 1964.

Bishop Brazier and Dr. Martin Luther King Jr. at a rally in Chicago, 1966.

Bishop Brazier and Rev. Jesse Jackson discussing jobs in construction trade in Chicago, 1969.

Bishop Brazier at the Woodlawn Organization's
steering-committee meeting.

Bishop Brazier at news conference on
gang program.

Bishop Brazier and President Clinton in Washington, D.C., 1994.

The Message Given to Him

9

The Message:
"Saved by Grace and Grace Alone"

*For by grace are ye saved through faith; and
that not of yourselves: it is the gift of God.*
— *Ephesians 2:8*
*Jesus Christ died that we might live; our sins
are forgiven; new birth changes our lives;
and eternal security comes as a result of
being saved by Jesus Christ.*
— *Arthur M. Brazier*

In the prologue to his book *Saved by Grace and Grace
Alone,* Bishop Brazier lays out the core of the message he
has been given:

> One of the most profound and captivating subjects in
> all the Bible is the Eternal Security and Final
> Perseverance of the saints of God. I have approached
> this subject with careful study and prayer. I've asked
> Almighty God for guidance and understanding — that
> my words would be seasoned — with the salt of the
> Holy Spirit, and my conclusions would be in harmony
> with the gospel of the grace of God.

This position is not one that was clear to him when he
was called but one that evolved as the Holy Spirit worked

with and through him. Bishop Brazier recalls that he once
accepted the Arminian position that a child of God could
lose his or her salvation if he or she sinned. He admits that
"in my earlier Christian experience, I heard about the
doctrine of eternal security. I didn't believe in it because it
wasn't taught to us. I was taught once you were saved, you
had to be very careful because you could commit some
kind of sin and still end up in hell."

Bishop Brazier heard this teaching and, in his obedience
to what he thought was the Word of God, followed it.
However, this line of reasoning did not make a lot of sense
to him. He was eventually able to move beyond rote
recitation because he had grown up with something inside
that nudged him when he was confronted with words or
deeds that were counter to what the Holy Spirit would have
him follow. He had learned through trial and error to be still
and to seek clarity when these inner stirrings arose. The
incongruence led him to "diligently study the Word of God."
He reported that in this process "certain Scriptures caught
my attention. For example, 'For by grace are ye saved
through faith; and that not of yourselves: it is the gift of
God,' and, 'Ye have not chosen me, but I have chosen you.'"
The research led him to "read not only the Holy Bible, but
the masterful works of other men — both pro and con."

The quest for a deeper understanding of the message he
was given to preach to the people of God led to three
variations of the same question: "Can a truly saved, born-
again person be lost again? Can a Spirit-filled person,
having received Jesus Christ as his personal Savior, lose his
salvation and eventually be cast into the lake of fire at the
great white throne of judgment? Can a person who has
been translated out of the kingdom of darkness into the
kingdom of God's dear Son be retranslated back into the
kingdom of darkness?"

Bishop Brazier views Christendom as being divided into
three categories on the subject of the "enduringness" of

salvation; there are those who believe a child of God can be saved and then can eventually be lost. This is a system of belief that teaches that Jesus Christ died equally and indiscriminately for every individual but that humans can successfully and finally resist the regenerating effectual power of the Holy Spirit if they choose to do so. Bishop Brazier points out that according to this system, which is called Arminianism, "even if [a person] accepts the saving grace of Jesus Christ, it is not necessarily permanent, because this system teaches that although a man may be ransomed by Christ and born again through the Holy Spirit, he may, in spite of God's wish and in spite of God's powerful effort to save him, throw it all away and perish eternally." Salvation is not an eternal, unconditional act of God for Arminians. It is partly based on human effort.

There are also those who believe that a person who is truly saved cannot be lost again. According to Bishop Brazier, these persons are called Calvinists. The Calvinist system holds that, as a result of the fall in the Garden of Eden, "man is completely guilty, corrupted, and hopelessly lost." This system "teaches that man is dead in trespasses and in sin and is by nature a child of wrath." Thus, "he is totally unable to do any meritorious work toward obtaining salvation …." Therefore, "he is totally dependent upon the grace of God." But once he is saved, he is saved forever.

The third system, Universalism, Bishop Brazier believes, has no scriptural foundation and has never been generally accepted by Christian churches. It teaches that Jesus Christ died for all and that, in the final analysis, every human being that ever lived will be saved, either in this life or through some activity of God in the future. Some adherents to this system even hold that Satan and all the fallen angels will eventually be saved.

The bottom line for Bishop Brazier in the teaching and preaching of the Word of God is that one who is called is not allowed to be governed by emotions, but "it is the duty of every teacher to subordinate his or her theories to the Bible and not [to] what seems to him or her to be true or reasonable, but simply what the Bible teaches." The one who speaks must be anointed and must have participated in theological education — whether it be formal or informal — in order to extract the meaning from the written Word of God.

Bishop Brazier sees the divisions created by doctrinal positions as unfortunate. He believes that they obscure the true teaching of the Word of God. When pressed for the label that best describes his style, he chooses to call himself a "Paulinist," because it was the apostle Paul who initiated the "saved by grace and grace alone" position. Bishop Brazier believes that Paul was an inspired writer who broke away from the legalistic bondage of the Old Testament. In the final analysis, whatever system one uses must be submitted to the Bible for judgment.

From his perspective as a Paulinist, Bishop Brazier focuses on three points of faith — the sovereignty of God, predestination and election, and man's free will. He sees these tenets as having bearing on the eternal security of the one who is a believer. According to Bishop Brazier, the sovereignty of God means that "God not only created the universe; he also rules over all he has created. God is absolute .... He possesses supreme power, unlimited in scope and extent .... He has undisputed ascendancy .... He is absolutely free. He is ever present, all knowing, all powerful and unlimited in any way whatsoever."

When one raises questions about the "fairness" of God — why he allows some to suffer while others appear not to, why all prayers are not granted, or why some have more than others — Bishop Brazier responds by reminding the questioner that "all things are not according to God's will and that some of the things that we witness are due to man's sinfulness. However, the results of sinfulness do not negate God's sovereignty. One who has and practices a strong biblical faith can survive the perils and misfortunes that eventually befall all humans."

Bishop Brazier is quick to remind listeners that none of us is in a position to judge the other and that "only God knows the true character and heart of the individual. However, there are some things we believe that may be problematic or even harmful to our spiritual growth, for example, the person who believes that if you become ill, it is because you did not have enough faith; whatever you want, if you have faith you will get it; or if you walk with God, you will be on easy street. These are erroneous ideas. Religion with this kind of an interpretation renders God no more than your servant. A God like that is not the God of the Bible."

In speaking of the sovereignty of God, Bishop Brazier is forceful about his disappointment in those who continue to use a "broken system that does not issue forth water." He speaks of those who do not turn to the sovereignty of God and instead choose a victim mentality and much lamentation about the white man causing the blight in the African American community. He says, "The focus should be on who is really creating the conditions under which we live." He uses several examples to make his point. "No one forces another to take drugs, to strew paper over the ground, or to paint graffiti on the walls."

He points out the one thing that can free people from self-imposed bondage when he says, "I am an old man; I am going down the other side of the mountain, so I speak to you about a lesson for the youth. Get your minds fixed on Jesus. All of us will have to cope with obstacles, problems, hindrances, temptations dogging at our footsteps, and disappointments hanging on us like our shadows. However, the one thing we have in common, no matter what our station in life, is that we are all one in Christ. What is given to us is the Holy Ghost so that the people can have power!

"Why did God deliver some men and women of faith

but did not deliver others; why were some killed and some not?" Bishop Brazier believes that "the answer to these questions is [that God] is sovereign, and being sovereign, he does what he pleases." He reminds us that "God bestows his mercy upon whom he pleases and when he pleases. Conversely, he withholds his mercy from whom he pleases, as it seems good to himself."

There is a kind of power in this response that reveals Bishop Brazier's belief in the sovereignty of God. However, it is infrequent that he gives a response that does not send the questioner off looking for ways to deepen his or her own understanding of the question — not because he assumes that all things are knowable but because much can be learned in the process of finding out that there is no humanly available answer.

Bishop Brazier often uses the Socratic method (leading the questioner into answering his or her own question), delighting in getting the questioner to generate further questions. His usual style is to quickly scan his sharp long-term-memory bank, remove his glasses, and pontificate a mixture of philosophical, theological, sociological, anthropological, and political possibilities.

One who dialogues with him gets the benefit of hearing answers that are both wise and spontaneous. He in no way tries to impress the seeker but tries to help him or her with the fullest possible response. His goal is also to suggest resources to which the seeker can turn to study the question further for him- or herself.

Bishop Brazier's book *Saved by Grace and by Grace Alone* is filled with wise observations and rich Scripture to support his Spirit-led scholarship on the issue of God's sovereignty. He ends the section on the sovereignty of God by indicating that the Bible declares emphatically and without equivocation that God is able to save us eternally. He believes that such a statement can be true because God "is at one and the same time omnipotent, omniscient, and omnipresent."

His belief in the sovereignty of God also helps the Bishop explain the relationsip of God and Satan. "The idea that Satan and God are struggling over souls is a figment of the imagination," he says. "Some people say Satan is fighting with God for souls; Satan wins some, and God wins some. If that be the case, then Satan is winning some, and, conversely, God is losing some. If these people are saying that God is losing souls, then they should stop singing the hymn 'Jesus Never Fails.'"

The second major tenet of faith for Bishop Brazier is the security of the believer. The core idea of this aspect of Bishop Brazier's message is that God's grace is never "undone" by human efforts. In other words, "if one has received God's grace, which is unmerited, how then can one lose that which was unmerited by [getting demerits — doing bad things]? The Bible makes it very clear that you cannot be saved by your works," Bishop Brazier says. Neither can you lose salvation by your works. The key to the position he takes seems to be the fact that salvation does not preclude the possibility, even the probability, that one will sin once he or she is saved, but he clarifies this point by indicating that "the Bible teaches us that he who is born of God does not commit or practice sin, for God's seed remains in him, and he cannot habitually live in sin because he is born of God."

The operative words in this statement are "practice" and "habitually." They suggest that the saved person does not become immune to what Bishop Brazier says is a unavoidable part of the human condition: sin. He goes on to say, "The Bible says that there is none good, no not one." Thereby the lofty perch of perfection on which some saved people choose to rest when they claim "eternal security" is eliminated.

Bishop Brazier on the other hand warns that belief in eternal security does not mean "that one can live a sinful life and still be saved." He contends with great persuasion that "nothing is further from the truth." On the contrary, "a person who has been truly born again can look back and see from whence God has brought him or her."

For many people, especially detractors, the problem in this doctrinal position appears to be in understanding the subtle yet powerful distinction between "living in sin" (practicing sin habitually) and occasionally committing an act of sin that we know is not consistent with the "new creature" we are struggling to become in our daily lives. In dialogue with Bishop Brazier it becomes clear that the legalistic or literalistic interpretations of the Bible do not allow room for a person to know that his or her change in consciousness through the working of the Holy Spirit is what will keep him or her from returning to the old "habitual" behavior — living in sin without self-recrimination.

The third major tenet of faith, according to Bishop Brazier, is predestination and election. Bishop Brazier sees predestination as teaching "that events come to pass because a wise, powerful, and holy God has decreed them. Predestination teaches that from eternity God has had one plan or purpose, which he is bringing to perfection. It teaches that the end of God's plan is his glory and the good of his people." Election for Bishop Brazier "refers to our being chosen by God as an instrument of his grace." To illustrate this point, Bishop Brazier writes, "God chose us before he created the universe, before the foundation of the world. Having chosen us, he foreordained us. He chose us not because he saw any good in us but because of the good pleasure of his will." Bishop Brazier sees no connection between predestination and election and fatalism.

He also raises the question of whether man is a free moral agent. He takes the reader of his book into a discussion of how one can balance man's free will against God's sovereignty. The crux of the argument is that the person chooses that which is according to his or her nature. Bishop Brazier contends that the person will choose righteousness only when there is intervention by the Holy Spirit.

"In matters of salvation, man chooses that which is according to his nature," he says. "Before he can choose or prefer that which is divine, there must be an intervention of the Holy Spirit, and a new nature must be given to him; in other words, he must be born again." The inability of humans to choose God without the Holy Spirit's intervention is related to the fact that humans are born with a sinful nature. To have "will" means one has the ability to choose, to refuse one thing and accept another. Bishop Brazier does not believe that people must lose their will in order for God to "save" them.

Preaching the message given to him — "saved by grace and grace alone" — often has meant that Bishop Brazier has come under criticism, because this doctrine is thought to make "people careless and indifferent about their moral conduct, their salvation having already been secured." He recalls once hearing a preacher say, "If I knew my salvation was eternally secure, I would go out and live in sin." To Bishop Brazier this kind of thinking "shows the abysmal ignorance of some people concerning the true nature of the new birth."

Bishop Brazier asks this question instead: "How can a born-again child of God, filled with the Holy Ghost, knowing that God has secured his salvation, deliberately live a life of sin?"

He contends that those who take the view of the preacher quoted above seem to think that "[eternal] security means one can continue to live the life of a sinner and still be saved based upon ... so-called acceptance of Christ as [one's] personal savior."

For the Bishop, the doctrine of eternal security "in no way" teaches "such an unscriptural position." The question that needs to be answered from Scripture is whether, when a person is saved, that person is immediately holy and entirely sanctified, conforming to the image of God — or not. Bishop Brazier does not take the denominational position on this question (most Pentecostals believe that saved persons no longer sin), nor does he accept a position based on the "edicts of men and church councils, but one based on the sacred Scriptures …." He cites two Scripture passages that apply to the question. He writes, "The possiblity of a sin being committed by a born-again believer is clearly seen in 1 John 2:1: 'My little children, these things write I unto you, that ye sin not. And if any man sin, we have an advocate with the Father, Jesus Christ the righteous.'" The more difficult text for him to explain is 1 John 3:9 — "Whosoever is born of God doth not commit sin; for his seed remaineth in him; and he cannot sin, because he is born of God" — and he explains away a perfectionism interpretation by saying that he believes the word "commit" is not an altogether accurate translation.

At the conclusion of his book, Bishop Brazier addresses the examination of Scripture used by Probationists to show that a person who was once saved can ultimately be lost. (Probationist is the term Bishop Brazier uses to describe a person who believes that one can be saved and lost repeatedly during one's lifetime.) Probationists believe that as long as one adheres to God's commandments, one is saved, but when one commits a sin, one is at that moment lost. One can, however, be restored to salvation through repentance and confession. Bishop Brazier often describes this position "as being saved on probation." He emphatically repeats that "the Scriptures do not ever say a child of God once saved can be lost again." To the contrary, he quotes Scripture as saying, without any reservation whatsoever, "… I give unto them eternal life: and they shall never perish."

Bishop Brazier indicates that Probationists often take Scripture out of context and in so doing call someone who may have a mere knowledge of Jesus Christ "a saved person." He does not see a person with mere knowledge of

Jesus Christ as being synonymous with one who is "born again." He notes that "there are many people who have a general knowledge of Jesus Christ," and he believes that "because of the general knowledge, they have escaped many of the pollutants of the world, but that does not mean they are saved." He goes on to indicate that such people can be found in all walks of life. "Some are ex-junkies and ex-drunkards who claim to be converted," he says. "Some are ordained ministers, yet they have turned to that which marks them as false teachers."

Bishop Brazier cautions against confusing enlightenment, which means "to be informed," with being "baptized into the body of Christ by the Holy Spirit." He contends that "countless numbers of people have been baptized and have gone to the prayer room, where inexperienced altar workers have thought they were filled with the Holy Ghost," and points out that "the more experienced altar workers have always recognized that many of these people have been blessed but have not actually been filled with the Holy Ghost." Therefore, his caution is to recognize that "being a partaker does not necessarily mean being indwelt, or filled, or baptized with the Holy Spirit."

Bishop Brazier calls upon all students of the Word to read objectively all the Scriptures relating to salvation and to seek to reconcile them with what the apostle Paul called "the gospel of the grace of God." He believes that through this effort they will discover that salvation is not a temporary state depending upon people but an eternal state depending upon God.

Bishop Brazier is neither dogmatic nor impatient with others who grapple with the concept of being "saved by grace alone." Even though it was the message given to him to preach to the people of God, he remembers that his own understanding came only after proddings by the Holy Spirit and long contemplative study.

The Effect of His Message

10

Building the Church

*A man who was hungry once told me that he
felt he could listen better to preaching that
was intended to fill his spirit if his stomach
was first filled. I knew then that the message
had to have impact beyond the doors and
the walls of the church!*

— *Arthur M. Brazier*

The least of what is required to build a church is bricks
and mortar. Rev. Elmer L. Fowler, founding pastor of Third
Baptist Church of Chicago and a contemporary of Bishop
Arthur Brazier, says that "the church grows and prospers
because of the pastor's belief in God and his ability to
follow the guidance of the Holy Spirit. Everything the
church has is a gift from God to the church."

On Easter Sunday 1963, Pastor Brazier was guided to
build a church. His first pastorship began in a house
church in March 1963 with 8 people and a treasury of
fourteen dollars. When he retired from actively pastoring
the congregation in December 1993, it numbered in excess
of 5,800 parishioners. As he received the vision of what he
was to do and what the church was to become, he inspired
the people he was called to lead until they became
empowered to become the kind of church they were called
to be — a church with a social-justice ministry.

Social justice and social action were at the core of the

message he was called to preach. He organized the Englewood Community Health Organization, established an emergency and transitional shelter program, and founded the Chicago Youth Club as part of his vision that the church should play a role in the total life of the community.

Rev. Fowler, when asked how a pastor who experiences phenomenal growth can make the transition from leading the small church to leading the large church, replied that "storefront" or "house church" psychology is only a problem for the pastor who is not being driven by the Holy Spirit. "There is no little church or big church; a church is a church. The pastor who prays, meditates, and asks God for guidance will receive what is needed to lead the people" through the different phases of church growth. "[A] pastor who is called is also given the vision, and if he or she follows the guidance of the Spirit, wherever the person finds himself or herself also can be found the instructions for the work to be done at that level."

Bishop Brazier indicates that for him the vision is very clear, but it came into focus in phases. "I can't say that these phases have been planned by me because I had such marvelous foresight, but, rather, as I look back over my pastoral life in this church, I can see God's hand," he says. As he recounts the growth, there is no reference to "I," but a constant flow of "we," the church: "[God] brought us from a congregation of eighty to a hundred people to twelve thousand," he says.

Bishop Brazier's belief in austerity led the church in phase one to pay off all the debt it had when he became pastor. He recalls three or four years of slow growth. "Then we started a continuous steady growth period, during which we paid off the mortgage and entered into a savings period in order to have a down payment for a new facility," he says.

Asked about the wisdom of building Pentecostal churches, Bishop Brazier responds that the Pentecostal movement has something tremendous to offer a world that "seems to have lost its morals." He believes that Pentecostalism has not been presented in a way that would attract the attention of large numbers of people from all walks of life. The Pentecostal church has a history of attracting people at the lower economic levels. Bishop Brazier reports that this was so prevalent that "[a] prominent minister advised me never to build a church in a middle-class neighborhood, because middle-class people did not want the Lord."

While Bishop Brazier was somewhat amused by this incident, his response indicates serious disagreement with his would-be mentor: "... I felt that the power of God and of salvation belonged to everybody and not just to the people who had less. So my vision was to reach out for this large segment of people that many Pentecostal churches did not feel could be attracted.

"....While the poor, as Jesus said, will always be with us, there is another group of people who are searching for something of [a] more spiritual quality, something that has greater depth. These are people who have or are achieving many of their educational and professional goals and consequently have disposable income to spend on pleasure, leisure, and recreation ...."

Bishop Brazier sees people with less money as tending to think that if they had more money their lives would be beautiful. Yet, he says, "I find that in [the] middle-class there is a yearning and hunger for a deeper relationship and a closer fellowship with God that they cannot find in the acquisition of material things." He shares his vision of reaching what he has identified as "this wide spectrum of people — from the poor to whoever they may be" because he believes that, as more people begin to develop in the church, "the resources of the church will begin to develop in such a way that it can reach out and do more for the community than we could ever do if we directed ourselves only to that class of people who seem to feel that the only hope for them would be heaven and that nothing is available for them here on earth. I think that our Christianity and our salvation have to do with more than just going to heaven."

He pauses here and reaches into his memory to pull up a story: "I am always reminded of that old saying about the bishop who was so heavenly minded that he was of no earthly use." Amused, he chuckles and says, "Heaven is the end of the journey, and the fruits that we have here are to be given to the people who are languishing without that spiritual relationship with God …. More and more I see people yearning and reaching for a spiritual depth that is now missing in the mainline denominations."

When Bishop Brazier speaks of the church, it is clear that he is not referring only to a physical structure. He sees the church as being like a hub in a wheel. "All the spokes that hold that wheel together find their origin in that hub, and they all go out and make the circumference," he says.

The spokes are representative of the church's various activities, interests, and concerns in all of life. He sees these activities as being centered in Jesus Christ, the hub. Therefore, nothing that is being done by the church should be a "detriment to the faith that we profess to have."

Bishop Brazier led his congregation in its decision to build a seven-million-dollar edifice on its existing site in the declining Woodlawn community. His vision for the church can probably be directly tied to the community of his youth. The African American community represented a cross-section of black life. Lawyers, physicians, teachers, bakers, domestics, and a horde of other nonworking, working, and professional people shared in the life of the community. It was out of this lived experience that he knew what the church could mean for people who were unable to flee from the urban experience. His call rooted him in the place where there could be diversity among the worshipers who were made equal in their quest for "word from the Lord." The homeless, substance abusers, professionals, working poor, seminarians, University of Chicago professors, believers, and "sinners" can all be found shoulder-to-shoulder on any Sunday morning.

The church needed to remain within the reach of the indigenous residents of the community. It was required by the message given its leader to invest its economic and human resources through its physical presence. Those who had become upwardly mobile and in a position to commute were called upon to make the conscious decision to continue to support the community in which this church was born. The Scripture "For unto whomsoever much is given, of him shall be much required" is one of the undergirding principles of the message preached by Bishop Brazier.

The Apostolic Church of God as a physical and a spiritual structure has repeatedly undergone the fires of transformation and has experienced rebirth on or near the original site. As the Holy Spirit deepened and broadened the pastor's vision, he in turn shared that vision with the people. The people of God have made this church a witness — spiritually, physically, socially, politically, and financially — in its community, where a holistic ministry is much needed.

11

Extending the Boundaries of the Church

*For I was hungry, and ye gave me food; I was
thirsty, and ye gave me drink; I was a
stranger, and ye took me in; Naked, and ye
clothed me; I was sick, and ye visited me; I
was in prison, and ye came unto me.*
                          — Matthew 25:35-37

Dr. David Daniels, assistant professor of church history at
McCormick Theological Seminary, raised a "chicken or
egg" question about Bishop Brazier's sharply honed
leadership skills. Did they emerge out of his community-
organizing experience, or did he come to that experience
fully equipped with the requisite administrative expertise?
Upon examination one would have to conclude that the
one sharpened the other. However, church-leadership
roles preceded his taking an active role in the Woodlawn
Organization (TWO) and the Center for Community
Change. As the pastor of a small church with few
resources, he learned how to operate a system from the
bottom up. He stoked the furnace, balanced the books,
paid the bills, and performed sundry pastoral duties.

Bishop Brazier came into this wide range of experience
out of both necessity and choice. In retrospect, he reports
seeing "the advantage that comes from having hands-on
experience through all of the phases of the growth of the
church. It is certainly an experience that keeps you humble

and in touch with the path traveled as well as with the one [God] who is really responsible for the progress."

In the process of the establishment and growth of his congregation, Bishop Brazier learned the discipline that comes from the necessity of having to be a "Jack of all trades." Coupled with his sense of being a leader and his early penchant to follow the Holy Spirit, the opportunity to manage a larger (community) system simply presented one more arena in which to live out his call to serve the people of God. Broader involvement in the community was particularly significant to Bishop Brazier because he interpreted his call to preach as being inseparable from a call to social justice and social action on behalf of the disinherited.

Bishop Brazier sees "nothing as [happening] in a vacuum." Historical realities of time and place and other circumstances are always present, even for pastors. He sees "Jesus as having established the model to be followed by clergy. Jesus went to the poor. He did not talk to them about personal salvation only. He dealt first with what the poor considered to be real in their lives. He dealt with their sickness, their leprosy, blindness, and hunger."

Bishop Brazier sees a direct link between the social ills that permeate society and the church's tardiness, reluctance, and failure in addressing them. He believes that "attempting to change the oppressive status quo is a matter not of tactics, but of principle ...." For him, at "a fundamental level every church is participating all the time in the oppressive status quo, either to change it or to uphold it or some mixture of the two ....

"This intertwined relationship [will] continue unless the church makes strenuous efforts to take the side of those who are trying to upset it for the sake of those who suffer under it," Bishop Brazier says. "If the church does nothing whatsoever and remains perfectly neutral, it will still be favoring the situation in this country as it is, including white racism." He emphatically believes "there is no possibility of not acting or not taking sides when it comes to the matter of the status quo."

Bishop Brazier sees some clergy and laity as viewing the preaching of the gospel as the church's only concern. He believes that people who take this position are viewing "man as two separate and distinct entities — soul and body …. They work with the soul of man [and only] for his eternal salvation. They feel it is the duty of the secular agencies of our society to provide for a man's material needs." For Bishop Brazier, their "withdrawal from the affairs of society" is tantamount to upholding and perpetuating the status quo.

As he does with any argument that he makes, Bishop Brazier turns to Scripture for support. He says that Scripture treats the body and soul as inseparable. There is concern in the Scripture for the whole person. Therefore, those who have been called to minister to the people should not separate their spiritual from their physical well-being. "A study of Scripture will show how much of biblical teaching speaks to living here and now, highlighted against a setting of history that is moving toward completion and Christ's coming again," he says. The position "I have nothing to do with … social problem[s]; I am here only to preach the gospel" finds no support in Scripture.

Bishop Brazier believes that "any church — whether it be Baptist, Pentecostal, Methodist, or [Roman] Catholic — that gives support to the immoral system of repression, by silence or by saying our role is only to preach the gospel and to save souls, is denying Christ and his clear teaching and example." He calls for "the church to lead the way in changing the status quo."

Bishop Brazier's involvement in community development also has a national dimension. In 1970 he worked with the nonprofit Washington, D.C.-based Center for Community Change (CCC). The organization focused on providing technical assistance to community organizations in the areas of community redevelopment and the empowerment of the poor. It conducted research under government contracts and published the results. Bishop Brazier is a former vice president in charge of a major-projects unit for CCC. His work with CCC allowed him to broaden his community-development work. He was "responsible for providing technical assistance to community-development corporations in various parts of the country," he says. "The focus was on urban projects. My involvement was a continuation of the struggle for balanced communities. Although I am no longer employed, I continue to serve as a board member."

Throughout Bishop Brazier's involvements in social justice and other social action, one thing remains constant: his call to preach the gospel. The places the call has taken him give meaning and form to the label "progressive" Pentecostal church leader. In whatever he believes and preaches, he finds his support not in what he as a man reasons out but in what he finds in God-given Scripture.

The preparation of others through mentoring serves as one way whereby Bishop Brazier can ensure the future of his vision both within his congregation and in the broader religious and social communities locally, nationally, and globally. Many are drawn to places where healing occurs. They seek the Word that soothes the brokenness they experience in a world with a diminishing spiritual core and the call for action that leaves people feeling at least somewhat empowered, as though they have some voice, at least about the small parcel of earth upon which they stand, sit, or lie.

The person with the healing Word draws others unto him- or herself because the hunger for the "living" Word is great in the land. James Forbes contends that the speaker of the Word, the one who is anointed, makes a difference. He or she is living proof that somebody cares — and perhaps even knows the way out the vast wilderness back into the arms of the loving Creator.

A pastor has a responsibility to mentor both clergy and laity. The major goal is to help them understand and interpret the gospel according to the doctrine espoused by the denomination to which they belong. For Bishop Brazier this position is influenced by his belief that the doctrine must have scriptural basis. But whom does the pastor choose to help him live out the vision and the message given to him for the people? One such person in Bishop Brazier's church is assistant pastor Elder Larry Martin.

Elder Martin describes his early life as "paralleling Bishop Brazier's. I grew up with a father I revered. My childhood was a time of nurturing and closeness." Today his walk with his pastor and mentor allows him to learn by example how one becomes a humble servant. Elder Martin is in a position from which he can watch Bishop Brazier as he moves through a day. Observing the Bishop entering storefronts or small churches (to attend or officiate at services) as if they were cathedrals has etched a picture of humility and grace on Elder Martin's soul. In these places Bishop Brazier greets the people and the pastors with all the respect accorded to those in a holy place. When he rides through the neighborhoods of his youth, he recalls the rich history he has lived. His history lessons are vivid, as though the events have just occurred. The younger man he has chosen to accompany him on the sojourn is warmed by the humanness of his mentor.

When asked why he was chosen for ministry in the church, Elder Martin replies, "I do not have a clue as to why Bishop Brazier chose me. All I know is that the opportunity to walk with such a humble man is in and of itself a learning experience. The perks that come from the spiritual and social exposures exceed what I would encounter anywhere else."

Dr. Horace Smith, an oncologist at Children's Memorial

Hospital in Chicago, is pastor of the mother church of the diocese, the seventy-five-year-old Apostolic Faith Church, "a fundamentalist flock" of two thousand. The church is described by its brochure as a "hand-clapping, foot-stomping, shout-raising Pentecostal congregation at 3823 South Indiana Avenue." Dr. Smith chose to become a physician and had a love for teaching, but he was called to preaching. He sees no disharmony between his roles as minister and doctor. He sees healing and faith as being parts of each other. Like Elder Martin, he feels enriched by his contact with Rev. Brazier, bishop of the diocese where Dr. Smith is a suffragan bishop.

Dr. Smith's first encounter with Bishop Brazier came when he was called to pastor Apostolic Faith Church. He recalls that Bishop Brazier was very frank: "He said, 'Dr. Smith, I am meeting with you because there are people at your church who are very influential; they feel like you are going to play a major role in your church, and they want your name recommended as a pastoral candidate. I am the bishop of the diocese, and your church is the mother church.'" In essence, he was being heard because he had been recommended.

Bishop Brazier, however, felt that the assistant pastor was a more likely candidate. He told Dr. Smith that he had nothing against him but that he did not know him and that his responsibility as the diocesan bishop was to the church. When the election took place, Bishop Brazier chaired it and declared the chosen one, Dr. Smith, the new pastor. Dr. Smith reports that they now laugh about the event and have become "very close."

Dr. Smith sees Bishop Brazier as having a tremendous influence on him. "He was the kind of minister that I always emulated," Dr. Smith says. "He was someone who I thought was committed to the Lord and to the people of God, someone you can trust." The respect the younger man has for his mentor is apparent as he adds, "When I became a pastor, he was there for me. He didn't try to direct me as pastor. He would say, 'You are the pastor; I am not; I am here to help you, but I am not going to try to give you my direction,' and he never did, but I knew he was always there. I could talk with him and so forth."

Dr. Smith recalls that Bishop Brazier has many dimensions. "He was always involved in the community," Dr. Smith says. "He never lost touch with people. He was a family man .... Those are the kinds of things that I look up to."

Dr. Smith also remembers some of the stories about Bishop Brazier's days in a struggling church: "I remember Bishop Brazier and his ministry when his church was not a large church. I remember when he was on Kimbark. He told me once, 'I had been the pastor for a couple of years; I don't know whether I had been discouraged or what .... I remember I preached every Sunday and taught every Wednesday for two years and no one ever got baptized ...."

It was this kind of sharing that endeared Bishop Brazier to Dr. Smith. It was a testament to how lightly the man wore the labels — elder, bishop, doctor — that had been bestowed upon him over time.

"People talk now about how massive the church is," Dr. Smith says. "I remember when Bishop Brazier had two hundred members, but he was committed to what he was doing .... He is not somebody who just fell into something. He worked, committed himself. So I think his views in ministry have ... evolved over time."

Dr. Smith feels that Bishop Brazier has received the most backlash from people within the denomination, many of whom see his eternal-security doctrine as being a loose one. Dr. Smith thinks that anyone who really listens to Bishop Brazier can hear a person who believes in sanctification and in people's spiritual lives reflecting that belief.

Dr. Smith believes that if the Holy Spirit is active in a person's life, that person will not engage in a life-style that is bereft of godliness. "In fact, one of the very telling [signs] of being [saved] is that your life speaks of Christ," he says. He thinks that some people have read Bishop Brazier wrongly and therefore have written him off. As a result, he believes, "Our organization has suffered because of [the underuse of the] tremendous abilities and experiences that he [Bishop Brazier] has to offer .... In many ways people have let this barrier blind them and not allow them to use [his abilities and experiences] in ways that I think could have been just so tremendous for our organization and for our churches." Dr. Smith cites Bishop Brazier's community- and organization-building skills as examples of what have been lost.

On this same subject Bishop Brazier reports, "I am beginning, especially among the younger pastors, to see some shifting in positions along the lines of accepting the eternal-security doctrine. I think in time they will begin to become more vocal on this issue and some of the other issues [prohibitions that are not scripturally based] that confront the denomination and ultimately society."

A compliment of the highest kind is paid a father when his son chooses to submit himself to his father's theological reflections and interpretations. If that son is also called into the ministry, the rejoicing of the father must be even deeper.

Elder Byron Brazier, assistant pastor and general administrator of the Apostolic Church of God and son of Bishop Brazier, left his home church to attend college and to live for a short time in a different state because of the demands of his high-level management job, not to follow another pastor, church, or religion. His father's congregation is what he has always called home. After returning to Chicago, he took over his father's Sunday-school class and has been able to sustain the class through his own teaching style. He in no way seems to be dwarfed by the big shadow his father casts. Even when he could use his father's influence to speed up transactions in the business world, he has decided "that a deal must be made based upon my ability to sell it."

Elder Byron Brazier believes that "one is affected by the call to public ministry, but how long it takes for one to answer the call no one knows. The Lord deals with this when he says this is what I want you to do." He feels that the action of the called one can be delayed due to a number of reasons.

"I never wanted to be a minister," he recalls. "I felt that I learned a great deal about the Bible from teaching Sunday school. I assumed the position of superintendent of the adult department of the Sunday school, but the Lord said, 'I want you to do more.' I felt directed to attend Moody Bible Institute but put off the decision to enroll because of job responsibilities."

In 1991 the push to act on preparation for the call became stronger, and he called Moody to enroll on what turned out to be the last day of registration. "All week long my desk had been filled with problems," he says. "They were marketing issues related to customer satisfaction. When I returned that day from Moody, they were gone. People kept coming in saying, 'This is fixed,' or 'This is OK.'"

In 1992 he knew that the call was indeed a call to public ministry. Elder Brazier reports, "Neither of my parents encouraged me along this path. They expected me to follow the leading of the Lord. Once the path was chosen, I was treated no differently than other ministers and evangelists in the church were treated. None of us receives preferential treatment. The Bishop asks them, male and female, to work according to their ability."

Elder Brazier's impressions of his father are described in words that are similar to those of others who are close to Bishop Brazier: "He follows the Scripture, attempts to model his life after the life of Jesus and the apostle Paul, separates out facts from opinions, serves others, believes in the work ethic, differentiates his own opinion from

Scripture, and lives a life that many others choose to emulate," says Elder Brazier.

Dr. Leon Finney, Jr., pastor of Christ Apostolic Church and director of the African American Leadership Partnership Program at Chicago's McCormick Theological Seminary, is another example of a person who was touched by the inclusive ministry of Bishop Brazier. "I received the benefit of Bishop Brazier's counsel in both my role as the director of the Woodlawn Organization and when I was making the decision about whether or not to attend seminary as a way to prepare for urban ministry," Dr. Finney says. "Over time, Bishop Brazier has shared with me the wisdom gathered by one who comes at any problem from a Spirit-led perspective. He is an eternal optimist who believes that the grace of God can turn the most adverse circumstances into a victory. Before making decisions in any arena, he examines the consequences on all sides. Through the excitement of the moment he wants to know the cost of the decision and whether or not it is consistent with the vision."

As Bishop Brazier prepares others, what are the plans for the future that he must consider? What is the magnitude of the legacy he will leave? What does he see for the Apostolic Church of God and for the broader Pentecostal church in the future? He is more than a visionary. He sees the vision, shares it with the people, waits until they are ready to move, and then invites them to help him bring it to fruition.

Has the message become too performance oriented? Too institutionalized? Is the focus too much on the personality of the Bishop? Or is the focus on the message he has been given and its impact on the church and its work in the community? Have the worshipers deified him, or do they see him simply as a vessel and not the Source? Do they hear his admonition to them when he says, "I am an old man going down on the other side of the mountain"? He moves with such agility, speaks with such assurance when they have trouble. How can they think of him as ever leaving them? Even when he had a job that took him away from the church and the city, he was back for Wednesday-night Bible study, and whoever heard of his missing a Sunday except when he has a serious excuse? One Sunday when he was hospitalized so many parishioners flooded the lobby of the hospital with prayers that he probably had no choice but to recover!

He missed a Sunday once when he went to Paris for two weeks, and he came back saying, "Never again." He got bored sitting leisurely in French cafes, reading and speaking as if he were a native. He missed the teeming life of the church. When he returned, the song that announced his entrance into the sanctuary, "Glad to Be in the Service One More Time," echoed what was in his heart.

Whose sight or vision matches or exceeds his? Do the people know he really is only a vessel fashioned by the Potter to contain the Word and that others are also prepared to carry on the dream, the vision, the work, the Word in the never-ending job of feeding the sheep of the Father?

The Bishop knows that he must ponder these questions, for his charge also includes some responsibility for the perpetuation, the "ongoing," of the message. It is certainly difficult to know how to come at such a challenge when his life has made an impact that exceeds even his own dreams.

What should he provide for those who must teach the young and the not-so-young? Surely they must glean from the past in order to maintain continuity, but only the wise can teach the lessons of the past in the present to those who will live in the future. When his congregtion can no longer sit at the feet of one they can see, they will sense his presence in the words and deeds that have become a part of his legacy.

Bishop Brazier sees his legacy as including "preparing the church's leadership to continue to be open to all who are seekers of liberation from the deep, dark things that hold them captive; dismantling the artificial walls that keep people out of the church; rebuilding the urban community in which the church sits; being of greater value in training the young people who must carry the message — saved by grace and grace alone — by example and word into the next century; and playing a more active role in the formal education of children. He says, "I am torn between creating a school in our own Christian tradition and supporting the existing public-school system. My greatest concern is that the cream not be siphoned off of the public system by the emergence of private schools. Therefore, a better place to invest resources may be in supporting the public-school system.

"I also envision institutionalizing a Christian-based counseling referral system and providing models for other churches that may want to replicate programs on smaller or larger scales. Developing a uniform new-members' training curriculum is high on [my] list [of priorities] because this may help them to feel more immediately a part of the church structure. Developing a cadre of leaders to assume positions in the auxiliaries without causing major disruptions within the church when someone leaves a position is also at the top of the list of my plans for the future."

Lest the life of the called and anointed one sound idyllic, consider the downside. When loneliness, fear, and doubt creep in between midnight and dawn when those who have a different call are sound asleep, who is the companion who will remain awake and watch and pray with the one who is revered during the day? Who can understand the weight carried by one chosen before the foundation of the world? If the called one is not careful, the "dark night of the soul" will consume him or her and leave the called one's being filled with bitterness.

Bishop Brazier puts into perspective this threat to the person called into ministry. He believes that when you "walk with God, sometimes you feel alone, but you are never alone. Jesus said, 'I will send you another comforter.'

Therefore, while one cannot stave off this feeling, a sense of return to empowerment and enlightenment are as near as the thought to call on the Holy Spirit for their restoration."

Being always in touch with both the power and the pain of the call and with the tension caused when one must minister to the whole person keeps the called one aware of the path he or she is treading. Why, then, would one knowingly choose this path? Rev. Reuben Sheares, the now-deceased pastor of the Park Manor Church once said, "Choosing Christ is the right choice, but it is not the easy choice."

Perhaps what is most important is the fact that the one who prays, studies, prepares, and waits for the guidance of the Holy Spirit is sustained through whatever the path holds. It also seems important for the anointed one to be aware that many will seek mentoring from him or her and that he or she must find someone who can reciprocate, someone who knows the terrain and can be a mentor to the anointed one. At Bishop Brazier's level there are few. Yet he is able to name one with whom he can speak the unspeakable — the unspecific doubt or fear that can envelop, without prior warning, a bishop of a twelve-thousand-member congregation as quickly as it can a minister of a fifty-member flock.

Even those who disagree with Bishop Brazier's theology or the doctrine that undergirds his call cannot deny his presence, power, and performance in the theological, intellectual, social, and political spheres. People like Timuel Black, professor emeritus, sociologist, historian, scholar, political activist, and contemporary of Bishop Brazier, help balance out the view that many who have known Bishop Brazier only since he has come into prominence may hold. Professor Black has had an opportunity to observe Brazier's work over the stages of its development. He regards Bishop Brazier as one who has earned respect in spite of and because of what he has done. He sees Bishop Brazier as intensely disciplined and focused on the calling and anointing of the Holy Spirit yet grounded enough in what is occurring in the world around him to know the reality of the struggle of the people, both the "churched" and the "unchurched."

The path of the called one is often a long, narrow, winding, unpaved road spotted with potholes. The traveler who accepts the call cannot avoid the condition of the road. But that traveler can find solace in knowing that along the road are way stations where the weary traveler can reconnect with the Source of the strength necessary to endure the journey. Furthermore, in the stillness necessary for this reconnection the traveler recognizes again that, regardless of the condition of the road, the Holy Spirit is ever present. Therefore, the trip can be made in spite of what may lurk along the way. Bishop Arthur Monroe Brazier has traveled and continues to travel this perilous path — from his own salvation, to the call and the anointing, to the service of others as they make their own journeys.

Looking back over more than seventy years, Bishop Brazier can see that his life has not been a series of coincidences or random events. Instead, he is able to make some connection between the preparation he underwent and the fruits of his labor in answering the call. When God calls a man and he answers, his life becomes a full-time struggle to develop the character necessary to live a life under grace.

Looking backward over the past, Bishop Brazier summarizes the effect of his having answered God's call: "While my life has not been free from the slings and arrows that have beset others, I feel assured that God's hand has been upon me. He has enabled me to lead the saints in Jesus' name through situations that I could not begin to understand at the time. However, I prayed and waited for guidance from the Holy Spirit. The answer allowed the puny creature that I am to receive, understand, share, and carry out the recurring message given to me by God — 'We are saved by grace and grace alone!' This message covers the spiritual and social situations that infringe upon the freedom of others inside and outside the walls of the church."

References

Barth, Karl. *Evangelical Theology: An Introduction.* 1963. Grand Rapids: Eerdmans, 1992.

Brazier, Arthur M. *Black Self-Determination: The Story of the Woodlawn Organization.* Ed. R.G. De Haan and R.F. De Haan. 1969. Grand Rapids: Eerdmans, 1982.

Saved by Grace and Grace Alone. 1987. Chicago: Saving Grace Ministries/Apostolic Church of God, 1993.

Browning, Don, David Polk, and Ian Evison, eds. *The Education of the Practical Theologian: Responses to Joseph Hough and John Cobb's Christian Identity and Theological Education.* Atlanta: Scholars, 1989.

Comblin, Jose. *The Holy Spirit and Liberation.* New York: Orbis Books, 1989.

Forbes, James. *Holy Spirit and Preaching.* Nashville: Abingdon, 1993.

Freire, Paulo. *Pedagogy of the Oppressed.* New York: Continuum, 1970.

Gramsci, Antonio. "The Intellectuals." *Prison Notebooks of Antonio Gramsci.* Ed. Q. Hoare and G. Smith. New York: International, 1994. 1-25.

Greenleaf, Robert. *Servant Leadership: A Journey into the Nature of Legitimate Power and Greatness.* 1977. New York: Paulist, 1991.

Hooks, bell, and Cornell West. *Breaking Bread: Insurgent Black Intellectual Life.* Boston: South End, 1991.

Jung, Karl. *The Archetypes and the Collective Unconscious.* 2nd ed. Trans. R.F.C. Hull. Princeton: Princeton UP, 1959.

Kelsey, Morton. *Caring: How Can We Love One Another?*
New York: Paulist, 1981.

May, Rollo. *The Meaning of Anxiety.* 1950. New York:
Pocket Books-Simon and Schuster, 1977.

Nouwen, Henri. *The Wounded Healer.* 1972. New York:
Image, 1979.

Thurman, Howard. *Jesus and the Disinherited.* 1949.
Richmond, IN: Friends United, 1981.

*With Head and Heart: The Autobiography of Howard
Thurman.* 1979. San Diego: Harvest-HBJ, 1981.

Tillich, Paul. *The Courage to Be.* 1952. New Haven:
Yale UP, 1975.

Colophon

Interior page design is by Aaron Phipps. Utopia type was set in 11 pt on 3 pt leading. This book was produced on a Power Macintosh 7100/66 and paginated with Quark XPress 3.31. The photos were digitally imaged in Adobe Photoshop 3.0. Film of the electronic pages was generated by Electronic Publishing Center.

M C M X C V

†